Indiana

A Bicentennial History

Howard H. Peckham

W. W. Norton & Company, Inc.
New York

American Association for State and Local History
Nashville

Author and publishers make grateful acknowledgment to the following for permission to quote from archival materials and previously published works:

The William L. Clements Library, University of Michigan, for permission to quote from the Thomas Gage Papers.

The Indiana Historical Society Library, Indianapolis, Indiana, for permission to quote from the letter of George Rogers Clark.

The Bobbs-Merrill Company, for permission to quote from *Travel Accounts of Indiana, 1679–1961,* by Shirley S. McCord, copyright 1970 by the Indiana Historical Bureau.

To Irving Leibowitz and Prentice-Hall, Inc., for permission to quote from *My Indiana,* by Irving Leibowitz, copyright 1964 by Prentice-Hall, Inc.

Library of Congress Cataloguing-in-Publication Data

Peckham, Howard Henry, 1910–
   Indiana.

   (The States and the Nation series)
   Bibliography: p.
   Includes index.
   1. Indiana—History. I. Series.
F526.P43   977.2   77–28308
ISBN 0–393–05670–8

Published and distributed by
W. W. Norton & Company, Inc.
500 Fifth Avenue
New York, New York 10036

Printed in the United States of America
1 2 3 4 5 6 7 8 9 0

Contents

Illustrations

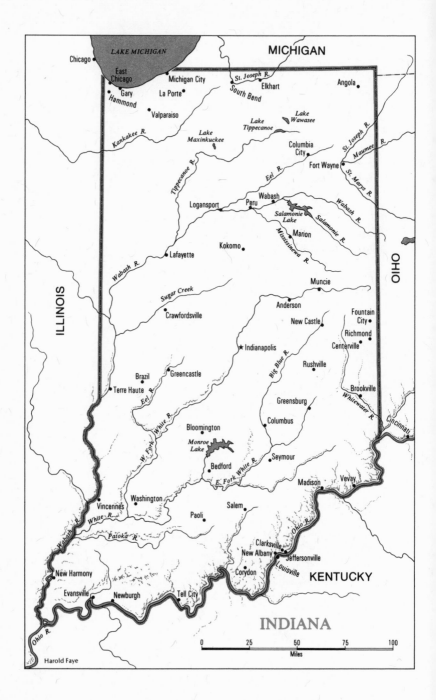

LAKE MICHIGAN

MICHIGAN

Chicago

East
Chicago

Gary
Hammond

La Porte

Michigan City

South Bend

St. Joseph R.

Elkhart

Angola

Valparaiso

Kankakee R.

Lake
Maxinkuckee

Tippecanoe R.

Lake
Tippecanoe

Lake
Wawasee

Columbia
City

St. Joseph R.

Maumee R.

Fort Wayne

St. Marys R.

Eel R.

Wabash

Logansport

Peru

Salamonie
Lake

Salamonie R.

Wabash R.

Wabash R.

Marion

Mississinewa R.

Kokomo

Lafayette

Sugar Creek

Muncie

Crawfordsville

Anderson

New Castle

Fountain
City

Richmond

Centerville

Indianapolis

Big Blue R.

Rushville

Brazil

Greencastle

Terre Haute

Eel R.

W. Fork White R.

White R.

Bloomington

Monroe
Lake

Greensburg

Columbus

Brookville

Whitewater R.

Cincinnati

Seymour

Bedford

E. Fork White R.

Madison

Vevay

Washington

Vincennes

White R.

Wabash R.

Patoka R.

Paoli

Salem

Ohio R.

Clarksville

New Albany

Jeffersonville

Louisville

Corydon

KENTUCKY

New Harmony

Evansville

Newburgh

Tell City

Ohio R.

Harold Faye

ILLINOIS

OHIO

INDIANA

0   25   50   75   100
Miles

Invitation to the Reader

IN 1807, former President John Adams argued that a complete history of the American Revolution could not be written until the history of change in each state was known, because the principles of the Revolution were as various as the states that went through it. Two hundred years after the Declaration of Independence, the American nation has spread over a continent and beyond. The states have grown in number from thirteen to fifty. And democratic principles have been interpreted differently in every one of them.

We therefore invite you to consider that the history of your state may have more to do with the bicentennial review of the American Revolution than does the story of Bunker Hill or Valley Forge. The Revolution has continued as Americans extended liberty and democracy over a vast territory. John Adams was right: the states are part of that story, and the story is incomplete without an account of their diversity.

The Declaration of Independence stressed life, liberty, and the pursuit of happiness; accordingly, it shattered the notion of holding new territories in the subordinate status of colonies. The Northwest Ordinance of 1787 set forth a procedure for new states to enter the Union on an equal footing with the old. The Federal Constitution shortly confirmed this novel means of building a nation out of equal states. The step-by-step process through which territories have achieved self-government and national representation is among the most important of the Founding Fathers' legacies.

The method of state-making reconciled the ancient conflict between liberty and empire, resulting in what Thomas Jefferson called an empire for liberty. The system has worked and remains unaltered, despite enormous changes that have taken place in the nation. The country's extent and variety now surpass anything the patriots of '76 could likely have imagined. The United States has changed from an agrarian republic into a highly industrial and urban democracy, from a fledgling nation into a major world power. As Oliver Wendell Holmes remarked in 1920, the creators of the nation could not have seen completely how it and its constitution and its states would develop. Any meaningful review in the bicentennial era must consider what the country has become, as well as what it was.

The new nation of equal states took as its motto *E Pluribus Unum*—"out of many, one." But just as many peoples have become Americans without complete loss of ethnic and cultural identities, so have the states retained differences of character. Some have been superficial, expressed in stereotyped images— big, boastful Texas, "sophisticated" New York, "hillbilly" Arkansas. Other differences have been more real, sometimes instructively, sometimes amusingly; democracy has embraced Huey Long's Louisiana, bilingual New Mexico, unicameral Nebraska, and a Texas that once taxed fortunetellers and spawned politicians called "Woodpecker Republicans" and "Skunk Democrats." Some differences have been profound, as when South Carolina secessionists led other states out of the Union in opposition to abolitionists in Massachusetts and Ohio. The result was a bitter Civil War.

The Revolution's first shots may have sounded in Lexington and Concord; but fights over what democracy should mean and who should have independence have erupted from Pennsylvania's Gettysburg to the "Bleeding Kansas" of John Brown, from the Alamo in Texas to the Indian battles at Montana's Little Bighorn. Utah Mormons have known the strain of isolation; Hawaiians at Pearl Harbor, the terror of attack; Georgians during Sherman's march, the sadness of defeat and devastation. Each state's experience differs instructively; each adds understanding to the whole.

The purpose of this series of books is to make that kind of understanding accessible, in a way that will last in value far beyond the bicentennial fireworks. The series offers a volume on every state, plus the District of Columbia—fifty-one, in all. Each book contains, besides the text, a view of the state through eyes other than the author's—a "photographer's essay," in which a skilled photographer presents his own personal perceptions of the state's contemporary flavor.

We have asked authors not for comprehensive chronicles, nor for research monographs or new data for scholars. Bibliographies and footnotes are minimal. We have asked each author for a summing up—interpretive, sensitive, thoughtful, individual, even personal—of what seems significant about his or her state's history. What distinguishes it? What has mattered about it, to its own people and to the rest of the nation? What has it come to now?

To interpret the states in all their variety, we have sought a variety of backgrounds in authors themselves and have encouraged variety in the approaches they take. They have in common only these things: historical knowledge, writing skill, and strong personal feelings about a particular state. Each has wide latitude for the use of the short space. And if each succeeds, it will be by offering you, in your capacity as a *citizen* of a state *and* of a nation, stimulating insights to test against your own.

James Morton Smith
General Editor

ACKNOWLEDGMENTS

Rather than another traditional state history, this book is one man's interpretation of what seems distinctive about Indiana, rising from its history. There is no attempt to be objective or detailed. My views are those of both an insider and an outsider. Nevertheless, any undertaking of such scope as this requires information and opinions—perhaps unpublished—from living persons. A number of old friends and new acquaintances have obliged me, and I am glad to acknowledge them.

Of foremost help were Gayle Thornbrough and Thomas Rumer of the Indiana Historical Society, Martha E. Wright of the Indiana State Library, Edward Zeigner of the *Indianapolis News,* Richard Simons of Marion, and the late Eli Lilly of Indianapolis.

They are followed closely by William E. Wilson and James Kellar of Indiana University; Earl Parks and Robert Topping of Purdue University; President John Horner of Hanover College; I. George Blake of Franklin College; Robert Conrad of the *Goshen News;* Howard Grossman of the *Salem Leader;* J. T. Rumbach of the *Dubois County Herald;* Ben Cole of the *Indianapolis Star*'s Washington bureau; former *Indianapolis Times* reporter Irving Leibowitz, of Marion, Ohio; Diane Lazarus of the Indianapolis Museum of Art; Al Bloemker of the Indianapolis Motor Speedway; Ward Brown of the Indiana High School Athletic Association; Dr. Alexander Moore of the Indianapolis Public Schools; Max Jackson of the Indiana State Chamber of Commerce; attorney Alan Nolan of Indianapolis; Loretta B. Glenn of Historic New Harmony, Inc.; J. Irwin Miller of Columbus; and Landrum Bolling of Lilly Endowment, Inc.

In addition to having questions answered by the Indiana State Library, I was well served by the Gary, Fort Wayne, and Madison public libraries.

Part I

1

In the Beginning Was the Word

AND the word was *Hoosier*. But neither it nor the distinctiveness of Indiana is easy to define. Except for the Ohio River coursing along the southern sole of this boot-shaped state, and the Wabash spilling down its lower lacings on the west, the boundaries are artificial—simply straight lines on a map. The visitor in an automobile or aboard a train does not know when he enters the state or when he leaves it, unless he sees a welcoming sign or a historical boundary marker. There is no change in vegetation or physical feature from adjacent states. The airplane passenger notices nothing different.

Indiana is also one of our smaller states, thirty-eighth in size, measuring 160 miles wide and averaging 265 miles in length north to south, embracing 36,354 square miles divided into 92 counties. All too frequently the traveler going a long distance regards Indiana as simply something to get across on the way from Ohio to the Mississippi River, or on the route between Chicago and Louisville. The northern half of the state is gently undulating, like northern Ohio, southern Michigan, and northern Illinois. The southern half is hilly, again like its bordering neighbors. No special geographical feature dominates the landscape, no mountains such as those that distinguish Colorado, no desert corresponding to that defining Arizona, no such great bay as that that shapes Rhode Island. The highest "peak" in Indiana is a hill near Lynn in Randolph County on the eastern border: 1,285 feet. Nor is there a special product associated with the state, such as autos in Michigan, citrus fruits in Florida, wheat in Kansas, beef cattle in Texas, potatoes in Idaho, or maple syrup in Vermont. Indiana has no symbol, projects no image.

Topography has had some influence on the human story. The last glacier covered somewhat more than half the state on the north, enriched its soil, cut its rivers, and scooped out some four hundred lakes and bogs along its upper reaches as it withdrew. The richest farm lands came out from under the ice in the broad central region, augmented by fertile acreage in the north, after swamps were drained. Not surprisingly, the northern half of Indiana is more prosperous than the southern half, if much less scenic. The thin soil and rugged terrain of the south precludes an agricultural domain, except for a fertile strip down the Wabash. The hills secrete soft coal, oolitic limestone, and clay deposits, but those same hills discouraged railroad development and hence industry. The narrow valleys and sharp ridges summon the gaze to enchanting vistas, and the color of foliage in fall and spring, along with minor waterfalls, delights the eye. For decades the landscape has inspired poets and painters. Rivers occasionally disappear, and great caves have been discovered, as well as mineral springs. Southern Indiana is beckoning country that haunts the natives who leave it. But industry favored the open country of the north, easily crisscrossed by highways and railroads.

The climate varies, but not so greatly as to produce wide differences in flora and fauna. Once the state was heavily forested, with 124 native species, mainly hardwoods. Except for an open prairie in the northwest, the land was almost covered with 17 species of oaks, a dozen hard and soft maples, yellow poplars, tough ashes, black walnuts, tall sycamores, spreading elms, stately gray beeches, and bountiful hickories. All of these were trees from which houses, barns, furniture, wagons, and rail fences could be built. Also familiar were locust, mulberry, sassafras, and wild cherry. In small supply only were the pines, a few in the south. Timber is still a valuable and renewable source for furniture and veneers. Dogwood and redbud are of limited use, yet are unsurpassed for their spring beauty.

There are even more varieties of shrubs, offering food and shelter for birds, small fruits for humans, and occasional medicines. They include the elderberry with its clusters of white flowers, bittersweet with its orange berries, the flaming sumacs, yellow and white honeysuckle, trumpet creepers, hazelnuts, and several wild berries. Smilax and ivy carpet southern areas. Slopes and meadows are lush with wild flowers of all hues and variety.

Kinds and amounts of animals have diminished, of course. Where there once were sixty-six species of mammals, about fifty remain—and in fewer numbers. Soft-eyed deer, red fox, squirrels, and rabbits are still hunted seasonally, and traps are set for muskrat, raccoon, and opossum. Bird species are seriously diminished, but still number more than a hundred. Waterfowl and marsh birds are found in the north; sparrows, robins, and cardinals abound, along with warblers, larks, bluejays, woodpeckers, swallows, and wrens. The watchful can spot red-winged blackbirds and wild canaries in the north, and orioles and indigo buntings in the south.

Geography affects the inhabitants because it determines the natural resources, the wild life, the crops, the transportation, and the location of towns, yet the absence of extremes in heights or temperature or fertility in the land that became Indiana allowed great freedom to the settlers in planning their own futures. If Indiana is not distinctively marked, geographically, it resembles more a vacant stage on which the actors could erect their own scenery, move about as they wished, and thus determine their own roles.

The Wabash River is associated completely with Indiana, though it rises in western Ohio and flows westward across the state before it turns southward. Little remembered is that it flows for five hundred miles, longer by a hundred miles than the convolutions of the Ohio in its distance along the southern edge of Indiana. Between them lies the White River, with two forks and several branches. On the eastern side of the state, the Whitewater River runs southward into the Ohio. Northward, above the Wabash, the Kankakee pours into Lake Michigan, along with the Calumet. In the central north is a watershed, or regional divide: all streams that flow ultimately into the head-waters of the Maumee at Fort Wayne and all those that reach Lake Michigan empty their waters into the North Atlantic via the St. Lawrence River. All tributaries of the Wabash, the White, the Whitewater, and the Ohio rivers go down the Missis-sippi and pour into the Gulf of Mexico.

All the congruity of land and climate, however, has not pro-duced a uniformity of agriculture. There are noticeable dif-ferences still between north and south, apparent to natives as well as to visitors. As one moves north from the center, the fa-miliar dominance of corn, hogs, wheat, soybeans, and tomatoes eventually gives way to dairying, extensive chicken and egg production, and muck crops of onions and celery. On the far-thest rim, another crop perfumes the air: peppermint and spear-mint. Two-thirds of those flavoring oils produced in this country used to come out of northern Indiana; one-fifth still does.

Here too is the summer-resort activity, with ninety-seven lakes in Kosciusko County and a hundred in Steuben County, for example. Farther west are the great sand dunes of Lake Michigan, making a magnificent playground. The fishing holes and canoe streams of the Indians have become the recreational retreats of the white man, whose vacation clothing has become as scanty as that of the red man.

In contrast, the extreme northwest, around the arc of Lake Michigan, is devoted to steel-making and oil refining so essen-tial to modern life, yet unfortunately darkening the landscape and polluting the air. Residents of the northern half of the state show a spirit of enterprise, alertness, and industry. Their new or remodeled farm houses and neat barns demonstrate that farming still pays. Their towns are bright and clean and busy, their houses usually well kept. Secondary roads are paved, the con-solidated schools are new and almost as large as the adjacent gymnasiums in this basketball country. The factories, seldom large, are relatively new and integrated to the landscape.

Below the old National Road, which stretched westward from Richmond, near the Ohio boundary, through Indianapolis to Terre Haute, almost bisecting the state, the region is less well-populated and farming is less rewarding; industries are scattered. The houses, with some glorious exceptions, are more modest, some of the stores more run-down. A few of the towns look seedy. The tax base diminishes, with its attendant deficiencies in roads and schools and services. If the people move more slowly, they are more friendly and patient. They step to a different drummer, or to no drum at all. And in every direction the hills, frequently reforested, show that man has made peace with his environment.

Indiana's neighbors tug at its borders. The northwest corner, the Calumet region, so heavily industrialized, is oriented around Chicago for shopping, marketing, and newspapers. It is in truth part of what the ubiquitous *Chicago Tribune* calls Chicagoland. Though Gary is Indiana's third-largest city in size, it is least Hoosier in character and not a center for any area. The southeast looks to Louisville and Cincinnati for urban delights. Only the northeast region, which centers on Fort Wayne, and the southwest, on Evansville (cities second and fourth in population in the state), retain some cultural independence. Indianapolis, the capital and largest city, stamps its identity on a vast central region. It is to Indiana what London is to England. These three contiguous areas, stretching diagonally from northeast to southwest, might be regarded as the true Hoosier state. Yet the last three cities mentioned, because they are populous, have more the characteristics of other cities in the upper Midwest than the flavor of Hoosierdom. That leaves the countryside and the smaller cities and towns to exemplify the state as it used to be.

Place names offer no focus and no clues to Hoosier character. They reflect many interests and the amorphous surface of Indiana. Indian names predominate in the north—Muncie, Kokomo, Mishawaka, Monon, Wakarusa, Kewanna, Nappanee, Winnemac, Shipshewana, Wabash, Tippecanoe, Wyandotte, and Lakes Winona, Maxinkuckee, and Wawasee. French names survive in Vincennes, Terre Haute, Busseron, Versailles, Orleans, Lafayette, La Grange, and La Porte. Natural features dictated such names as Twin Lakes, Beech Grove, Dogwood, Laurel, South Bend, Flat Rock, Sulphur Springs, French Lick, Rolling Prairie, and Clay City. The classical revival of the early nineteenth century introduced such names as Memphis, Rome, Troy, Athens, Attica, Delphi, Mount Olympus, Syracuse, Carthage, and such biblical names as Nineveh, Samaria, Goshen, and Canaan. The Mexican War prompted commemoration of battles in Monterey, Vera Cruz, Cherubusco, Jalapi, and Saltillo. Latin America furnished such other names as Brazil, Peru, Cuba, Mexico, and Valparaiso. If our presidents from Washington to Van Buren are preserved in town names, they are outnumbered by sixteen places named for saints. The American Revolution and military aftertimes are recalled by Bunker Hill, Saratoga, Monmouth, Yorktown, Fort Wayne, and Waterloo. Then there are literary allusions, largely forgotten, in Metamora, Waverly, Priam, Homer, Banquo, and Hymera. Corydon was named for the shepherd in William Henry Harrison's favorite song. Romona is taken from the title of Helen Hunt Jackson's novel, but misspelled. Nostalgia for places left behind may be seen in New Albany, Plymouth, Richmond, Boston, New Philadelphia, Bennington, and Hagerstown. In this potpourri, local heroes are not forgotten: Clarksville, for George Rogers Clark; Tipton, for General John Tipton; Poseyville, for Governor Thomas Posey; Connersville, for pioneer John Conner; and Evansville, for Robert Evans. Scircleville is not a misspelling, but honors the founder, George Scircle, while Trevlac is named for one of its founders, a Mr. Calvert—spelled backwards.

An Indiana distinction is the local pronunciation of some of the names. It is *Bray*-zil, *Pee*-ru, *Lay*-fee-ette, *Vy*-go County, and *Chy-lie*—both syllables stressed equally. The Swiss who settled on the Ohio in southeast Indiana came from Vevey, pronounced Ve-*vay*. To preserve that pronunciation in Indiana, they spelled it Vevay. To no avail! Hoosiers call it *Vee*-vee.

Like Kentucky, Indiana has its share of odd names—Pin Hook, Fickle, Gnaw Bone, Popcorn, Stony Lonesome, Surprise, and Santa Claus. There is even a deep hollow called Pike's Peak. A westward-mover appeared in Brown County (another version has it a local man starting west) with a covered wagon on which he had bravely painted "Pike's Peak or Bust." Well, he busted and was reduced to selling a variety of belongings. If something unusual was wanted, the local advice was "Better see that Pike's-Peak feller." And so the name became attached to his camping place.

There is also a Dublin in eastern Indiana. Several years ago a newspaper feature story pointed out that there were no Irish in this Dublin. True, but irrelevant: the town is called Dublin only because of slurred pronunciation. Once upon a time it was a stagecoach stop between Richmond and Indianapolis. As a station, it consisted of two log cabins, connected, where travelers might refresh themselves in the "double inn."

Some people declare that Indiana is invisible. Possibly so. The Indiana charm—except for some lovely scenery in several southern counties—is not apparent to the visitor or the distant consumer. You have to live here a while to gain a sense of what gives the state character. It is the people. This book is an attempt to tell what made them as they are.

Indiana is not one of the original thirteen colonies, of course, nor a child of one of them from old charter claims. It remained on the edge of the theater of war in the Revolution. It was not founded for a cause, as Kansas was, in the struggle between free and slave states. Its name acknowledges that here in the great Northwest was Indian country that would achieve its own identity. The first settlers were not fleeing British religious persecution nor any American political repressions. They were a post-Revolutionary generation of full-fledged Americans, imbued with all the freedoms earned on the tidewater, and exultant in their hopes. They migrated for the purpose of improving themselves economically while maintaining what their parents and grandparents had won. They were not starting over, but starting up.

Since those settlers were not escaping from a troublesome or intolerable life, they intended to perpetuate many ideals of the new United States. On that view there must have been general agreement, rather than antagonistic factions. The "movers" or newcomers tended to be fundamentally alike in outlook and allegiances. They believed in the perfectibility of mankind, and they glimpsed the Promised Land over the mountains. They were dissatisfied only with themselves and their personal prospects back home. In a hospitable new territory such as Indiana, they confidently expected to do better, to develop a life not simply rewarding, but fulfilling, one they could view ultimately with pride and a sense of accomplishment.

There was no Moses leading them into or out of the wilderness. They came by their own initiative, sometimes alone, more often in families, occasionally in groups. A few, suffering bad luck beyond their control or not understanding what a conquest of the wilderness demanded, would fail. They would go back east or move on to Illinois and Missouri or sink into despair and degradation where they were. But the vast majority would find in varying degree the Promised Land they sought. They would improve their standard of living and adopt rising expectations while they reared their children, until finally they would gather at Old Settlers' picnics to reminisce about the early times of exhausting labor, real dangers, minimum comforts, saddening illnesses and deaths, and the slow struggle that endeared this state of Indiana to them. If not secure according to today's standards, they didn't know it. They had erected sturdy houses, developed farms and businesses, created family ties along with political, religious, and educational institutions, and accumulated traditions. They possessed a heady sense of achievement. As early as 1831 a handful of the contemplative had come together to preserve a story they considered remarkable by forming the Indiana Historical Society. It would not celebrate hereditary position or recognize a new elite, but simply gather and record what the new generation, now old, had endured and overcome. Whatever they once were, wherever they had come from, they were already committed Hoosiers, here to stay. A conceit, perhaps, but they knew that the rising generations of Hoosiers, if they should not venerate the pioneers, could at least learn from their trials and mistakes and triumphs.

That appellation *Hoosier*—where did it come from? Various explanations have been offered, more ingenious than real. One version is that in 1825 a contractor named Samuel Hoosier or Hoosher was building a canal around the falls (actually, rapids) of the Ohio. He preferred to hire most of his workers from the north bank, or Indiana side, of the river, and they became known as "Hoosier's men" or simply "Hoosiers." The name stuck to them.

Another theory advanced is that the word is a corruption of the pioneer's greeting to those visitors who knocked on his cabin door: "Who's yere?" he called. Maybe he did, but should he not have said "Who's there?" rather than the illogical "Who's here?"

James Whitcomb Riley, the Hoosier poet, invented a more preposterous explanation. After referring to the pioneer penchant for brutal fighting, which included biting ears or noses and gouging out eyes, he told of a stranger entering a southern Indiana tavern after such a fight. Noticing a piece of human flesh on the floor, he pushed it with the toe of his boot and inquired, "Whose ear?"

The best explanation is more prosaic. Probably *Hoosier* is derived from the word *hoozer* in the Cumberland dialect of Old England, embodying the Anglo-Saxon root *hoo,* meaning *high* or *hill.* In Cumberland, the word *hoozer* denoted anything unusually large, presumably like a hill. By extension it was attached to a hill-dweller or highlander and came to suggest his roughness and uncouthness. Emigrants from Cumberland, England, settled in the Carolinas and spread to Georgia and Kentucky. They gave their name to the Cumberland Mountains, the Cumberland Plateau, the Cumberland River, and Cumberland Gap—even to the Cumberland Presbyterian Church. Thus, throughout the Southeast in the eighteenth century, *Hoosier* was used generally to describe a backwoodsman, especially an ignorant boaster, with an overtone of crudeness and even lawlessness. It was a synonym of *Cracker* and was eventually displaced by that word in Georgia and Florida. There were recognized Alabama Hoosiers, however, as late as this century. In short, it was a word that could be attached to a certain class of inhabitants in several states.

But the settlers of southern Indiana fell irrevocably under the denomination of Hoosier. The term was fastened here by the popularity of John Finley's poem *The Hoosier's Nest,* written about 1830, he said, and published January 1, 1833, as the carrier's address (distributed as a New Year's greeting) in the *Indianapolis Journal.* Obviously the word was widely familiar then or Finley would not have used it, although he spelled it *Hoosher.* The poem began:

> I'm told, in riding somewhere West,
> A stranger found a "Hoosher's" nest,

and, after describing the family cabin and its simple furnishings,

> One side was lined with diverse garments,
> The other, spread with skins of varmints,

ended with approval:

> In short, the domicile was rife
> With specimens of "Hoosher" life.

Before 1833, the word *Hoosier* had been used in an Indiana diary of 1827 and in a letter of 1826 as a familiar term for Indianans; specifically, it was written "Indiana Hoosiers." Indeed, there were variations of it. In the 1830s, a *Hoosieroon* was the child of Hoosier parents; and in the 1840s, a *Hoosierina* was a woman or girl who lived in Indiana. Those terms have not persisted—fortunately—but *Hoosier* endures.

If at first it was an uncomplimentary word, shouted in derision—as were *Quaker* and *Shaker,* originally—the early settlers of Indiana wore it as a badge of identification. Soon they called themselves Hoosiers proudly and even defiantly. The word might indicate that a man was rustic, but at the same time he was a virtuous yeoman of Jeffersonian standards, neither ignorant nor ill-mannered. In fact, Indianans who moved on to other states almost never denied their heritage. They readily announced to new neighbors that they were Hoosiers. Those who leave the state now seem not to lose their allegiance to Indiana, their sense of once belonging to a certain place. They can grow sentimental, even lyrical about it.

It can be argued that the great Miami chief Little Turtle was the first self-conscious Hoosier. He lived at Kekionga, near which Fort Wayne was built in 1794, and he was convinced that his tribe held ancient title to the Great Lakes region. When Constantin F. Volney, French traveler and historian, interviewed him at Philadelphia in 1798 and showed him a map to explain how Indians originated in Asia, migrated to Alaska, then drifted down through western Canada and across to the Great Lakes, Little Turtle listened dubiously. Why, he asked, could not the red man have originated where he lived and migrated to Asia? Could the State Chamber of Commerce have said more?

In 1919 William Herschell, columnist for the *Indianapolis News* and poet in the Riley tradition, came upon an old man near Knightstown who was sitting on a log in the warm sunshine and fishing in the Big Blue River. With a sweep of his arm to encompass the countryside, the old fellow exclaimed, "Ain't God good to Indianny?" Our poet was immediately inspired. He wrote thirty-six lines in three verses praising the beauty and serenity and superior virtues of the state. Each verse ended with a rhetorical question:

> Aint God good to Indiana?
> Aint He, fellers? Aint He though? [1]

What the poem demonstrates is that, despite the artificial boundaries, the variety of place names, the pleasant though nondistinctive landscape, and the jibes of outsiders, Hoosiers have a sense of place. They know what Indiana means to them.

1. *Indianapolis News,* May 31, 1919.

2

Hoosiers as Fighting Pioneers

$\mathcal{C}$ONFLICT shaped the beginnings of Indiana. Different races and different nationalities contended for domination of the area that was to become an American state. Frenchmen moved in among the Indians and brought Negroes with them. Englishmen followed and fought both French and Indians. Americans next appeared to combat the English and Indians, at three different times. How these constituent bodies grew or withered, intermarried or remained hostile, explains the amalgam that became Hoosier. Out of that long and shifting struggle emerged an identity.

There may have been relative peace among the prehistoric inhabitants—we simply don't know. How early Indiana was occupied by human beings is befogged in antiquity. Man was present in North America at least thirteen thousand years ago. He had come out of northeast Asia after the last glacier receded, crossed the Bering Strait, and drifted south and east. Almost nothing is known about these early red men except that they used a long, fluted projectile point on a spear. They were hunters and food gatherers, always moving. Some of those distinctive projectile points have been found in the Ohio River valley and up the Indian tributaries. They have not been dated.

The first major cultural stage that has been roughly dated by archaeologists falls in the period of 8000 to 1000 B.C. Indians of

14

that time were still hunters, fishers, and gatherers of mussels, berries, roots, and nuts. They used fire and made spears, stone axes, knives, and scrapers, along with bone fishhooks and drills. Probably they lived in caves temporarily, but they cultivated no gardens, made no pottery, and had no bows and arrows. Through the millennia, they adapted more efficiently to their environments. Hundreds of sites in the late Archaic tradition are found in Indiana, indicating an increased population. Mussel shells left after the meat was extracted created mounds, sometimes fifteen feet high and covering more than an acre. Fire pits contain some of their tools, as do their human burial sites. Occasional copper beads are found and the mysterious slate birdstones, carved in stylized effigy of a bird. Evidently human groups were learning to trade.

The next cultural tradition to be distinguished is called Woodland and extends from about 1000 B.C. to A.D. 900. It is marked by the appearance of pottery decorated with cord impressions and by rather specialized burial practices. Further, plant cultivation was introduced. The early Indian standard of living was on the rise, both with an improved and varied diet and with more utensils and tools. Their large burial mounds are found throughout Indiana, the earliest ones including the Nowlin Mound in Dearborn County (southeast) and the Stone Mound in Shelby County (farther north). Of later date are mounds in Warrick County, in Greene County, and up the Wabash Valley. A whole village and several burial mounds have been located in Posey County, in the corner where the Wabash empties into the Ohio. In the Kankakee River valley of northwestern Indiana are a number of mounds and camps of the Middle Woodland period. Mounds State Park near Anderson contains a circular mound 360 feet in diameter, three violin-shaped heaps, and two other low mounds. Twenty miles southeast, near New Castle, is a similar group of a dozen mounds. They are difficult to assign but seem to be Middle Woodland. Late Woodland mounds, containing a few artifacts and simple pottery vessels, are found in the southwest. Ceremonialism seems to have declined, but the bow and arrow appeared.

The last and most complex culture is called Mississippian and is dated A.D. 900 to A.D. 1500. It is marked by intensive cultivation of corn, beans, squash, melons, and other foods, which in turn required and permitted community settlements. Implements, utensils, tools, weapons, and ceramics (bowls, jars, bottles, some of them painted) show greater variety and survive in larger quantity. Clay, stone, wood, bone, shell, and copper were being used. Village remains suggest there was some political organization, as well as religious ceremonies. The finest example of this tradition in Indiana is the Angel Mounds on the flood plain of the Ohio near Newburgh, a few miles east of Evansville.[1] The site covers more than a hundred acres. The river forms one boundary, and a log stockade enclosed the other three sides. Near the center of the village is a large mound measuring 659 feet by 300 feet by 44 feet high, constructed in three terraces and flat on top. It must have been the habitat for a chieftain or an elite group. An open plaza faced it on the west, and at the far end was a temple mound. Around the plaza were large and substantial houses made of upright posts covered with mats and daubed with clay. Perhaps there were 200 houses and a population of at least a thousand residents.

The people capable of this culture at Angel Mounds were newcomers, not Woodland Indians who had grown more skillful. They appeared about A.D. 1300, and some groups also moved up the Wabash River. They may have been of Muskhogean or Siouan linguistic stock. Probably they came from the south, for reasons not known, and before 1500 they migrated back south, again for reasons not clear. Perhaps they reduced the fertility of the soil by constant corn-planting; perhaps they ran short of nearby timber for building; perhaps hostile hunting Indians were coming near. Whatever the disturbance, they left—and Indiana fell vacant.

As the seasons came and went, wildflowers bloomed and

---

1. Named for the owner of the farm when it was purchased by the Indiana Historical Society in 1938. With perfect appropriateness, Mr. Angel then moved to Paradise, Indiana.

faded as always, though they went unnoticed. The verdant hills and wooded plains gave cover to mammals and birds no longer hunted by man. The rivers, noisy and silent, still sought the far-off seas, while their fish swam uncaught. This Eden, replenished, calmly awaited new invasion—first by other red men whom we can more readily identify, then by white men about whose origins there is little mystery.

Not until after the middle of the seventeenth century did new Indians enter Indiana. The Miami drifted down from Wisconsin around the head of Lake Michigan, and were followed by the Potawatomi. The Kickapoo and Wea came across northern Illinois and pushed the Miami farther east. The Wea settled on the upper Wabash, the Kickapoo followed the Vermillion River down to its juncture with the middle Wabash, and the Piankashaw and Mascouten appeared around Vincennes. The Miami moved into western Ohio and up to the Detroit River, where, in 1708, they quarreled with the Sieur Antoine de la Mothe Cadillac at Fort Pontchartrain and fell back to the headwaters of the Maumee River. The southern two-thirds of the state was a vast hunting ground for the Shawnee of Kentucky, until the Delaware penetrated the eastern White River valley after 1715. Did this casual occupation mean that the land belonged to them? Were they the legal owners? Were there boundaries the tribes respected? These questions would be argued again in the middle of the twentieth century.

In the northern and extreme western parts of the future state, the tribes formed villages, where the women cultivated gardens, reared the children, made clothing and moccasins, and prepared the meals, while the braves hunted, fished, gambled, and made war. For these vocations they had to manufacture weapons, clay pots, tools, ornaments, canoes, and medicines; they also were concerned with placating the gods and preserving oral traditions. The gradual appearance of the French traders gratified them, because the white newcomers raised the Indians' standard of living. The Indians could barter furs for metal pots and pans, wool blankets, ruffled cotton shirts, iron tools, steel knives and traps, jews' harps, paint, and muskets that made their hunting more effective. They also gained access to French brandy and French diseases, paying a physical price that ultimately offset all the advantages of this technologically superior culture.

By 1744 the mix of peoples that was to constitute Indiana was already visible. Indians were preponderant; a few Negroes had been brought in; and two groups of Caucasians had arrived: the French, precariously settled, and a few adventurous Anglo-Americans furtively paddling the rivers of the wilderness in search of furs. A census ordered by the governor of Louisiana in 1744 revealed 40 Frenchmen and 5 Negroes at Vincennes, neighbor to about 150 Piankashaw. Farther up the Wabash at Fort Ouiatenon—the first white settlement in Indiana, four miles west of West Lafayette—was a score of Frenchmen amid a sea of Wea and Mascouten. At Fort Miamis (Fort Wayne) was a similar number of French and more than a thousand Miami.

French explorers had first entered the boundaries of modern Indiana in the 1670s, just after the Indians began drifting in. The Jesuit explorer and missionary Father Jacques Marquette spent the winter of 1674–75 near what is now Chicago and in the spring circled the head of Lake Michigan to go northward back to Mackinac Island, but he died on the eastern shore of the lake. Next to come was the Sieur de La Salle, heading for the Mississippi to determine its length and outlet. In December 1679 he and his party followed the eastern side of Lake Michigan southward to the mouth of the St. Joseph River. From there he proceeded up the river, made a portage near its "south bend" to the Kankakee River, and continued westward on the Illinois River. On his return journey the following year, La Salle probably recrossed the northwest corner of the future state.

Settlement was not yet attempted, but the English disputed even the French trade relations with the Indians of the western Great Lakes and Illinois country. La Salle tried to organize the western tribes against English invaders. The international wars for empire between England and France that began in 1689 did not end until 1763, with a treaty that left the English victorious. During that period of conflict, the French had tried to strengthen their control of the western region by a fort on the Detroit River in 1701. Then they discovered the Maumee-Wabash route to the lower Ohio River and the middle Mississippi, which turned their attention to fortifying that shorter passageway to the interior.

François-Marie Bissot, the Sieur de Vincennes, lived at Kekionga ("blackberry patch"), the principal town of the Miami on the site of modern Fort Wayne. He served as agent to keep the Miami trade confined to the French and to discourage any contact with Englishmen venturing over the Alleghenies. The town was a strategic spot because it commanded a ten-mile portage to Little River, which flowed into the Wabash and carried canoes to the Ohio and westward. Or at Kekionga canoes could go up the St. Joseph River and make a short portage to that other St. Joseph of Lake Michigan for northern travel. In 1717 a French officer, a dozen soldiers, and four licensed traders were sent by the governor of Canada to establish a small fort among the Wea on the Wabash, below modern Lafayette. This post, Fort Ouiatenon, the first white settlement in Indiana, remained for ninety years; it is older than such places as Savannah, Georgia; Richmond, Virginia; Pittsburgh, Pennsylvania; Buffalo, New York; Cleveland, Ohio; or any town in Kentucky or Tennessee. Beyond it, the Kickapoo were settled on the Wabash near the mouth of the Vermillion River. In 1719 Vincennes died at Kekionga, and the Canadian governor sent a replacement in 1721 to erect a fort there, which he called Fort St. Philippe des Miamis, but it became generally known as Fort Miamis.

The French governor of Louisiana was also interested in establishing a post on the Wabash. He assumed that his jurisdiction extended northward into the Illinois country and to the *terre haute,* or high ground, of the middle Wabash. Accordingly, he commissioned the able son of the Sieur de Vincennes as a lieutenant to take some Wea from Fort Ouiatenon downriver in 1732 to a new location within Louisiana's vague boundary. Young Vincennes began building a fort on the site of the present town named for him. He reported there were near him four Indian villages (Piankashaw) that were already trading furs to the English. He expected to change all that.

Since the Louisiana governor was making war on the Chickasaw around western Tennessee, he sought help from the northern tribes. Both Vincennes and the commandant of the Illinois country were ordered to rendezvous near modern Memphis in March 1736 with all the soldiers and Indian braves they could bring. They obeyed the summons and then found that the governor and his force had been delayed at New Orleans for lack of supplies. The two northern lieutenants led an attack on a Chickasaw village anyway, were routed, and both they and a Jesuit priest were captured. After suffering horrible tortures, all three were burned at the stake.

The Vincennes post was stunned by the loss and reduced in French and Indian settlers. Although a new commandant was appointed, the place dwindled to a minor fur-trading depot, and the local French turned to farming. Venturesome English traders from Pennsylvania reached the Miami and the Wea, as well as the Piankashaw, in 1750. In 1757 Vincennes had seventy-five inhabitants and three mills. The next year the Louisiana governor reported forty troops in the garrison and about twenty *habitans* who raised wheat, corn, and tobacco. The figures can't be reconciled unless there were, among the twenty civilians, men who had wives and children.

The French and Indian War finally turned in favor of the English. The whole of Canada was given up to the British in 1760. Meanwhile, the English agent, George Croghan, had invited all the Indians as far west as the Wabash to meet with him at Fort Pitt. About a thousand Indians turned up, including Miami, Potawatomi, and Kickapoo from Indiana. They could not afford to stay on the losing side. Croghan promised them a lucrative trade for their furs, a gunsmith to repair their muskets, and plenty of powder and lead for hunting.

As soon as the French surrendered Canada, General Jeffery Amherst sent Major Robert Rogers to take over the Great Lakes posts. Rogers received the surrender at Detroit and detached two parties of his Rangers to garrison Fort Miamis and Fort Ouiatenon. Vincennes was not affected, because it was part of the French Province of Louisiana, whose fate had not yet been decided.

A survey in 1762 showed 230 Miami braves at Kekionga, and the fort under Ensign Robert Holmes with a garrison of 15 men. There were 200 Wea, 180 Kickapoo, 90 Mascouten, and 100 Piankashaw adjacent to Fort Ouiatenon, where Lieutenant Edward Jenkins commanded a garrison of 20 men. Vincennes was still in French hands, but in the formal peace treaty of 1763 all of Louisiana east of the Mississippi was ceded to the British as well.

The French commandant left Vincennes in 1764, putting the settlement under the jurisdiction of local militia officers. So ended eighty-five years of French influence and control in Indiana, the Great Lakes region, and the Ohio Valley. The French had raised the standard of living for their Indian friends by rewarding their hunting and trapping, but they also gave them their diseases and liquor, which in the end debilitated the red men. Still preserved was the wilderness. It might have renewed the Indians, had they been left alone. But Englishmen succeeded Frenchmen, and settlers eventually followed traders. The Indian free way of life was doomed.

With the French soldiers gone, the Indians were learning what it meant to have British troops at the forts. General Amherst had ordered the strictest economy, now that war was over, and Indian help need not be sought or bought. There were to be no more gifts, and no more free powder such as the French had allowed, and no liquor at all. Amherst considered the gifts to be bribes, the powder to be part of the Indians' cost of hunting, and rum the cause of quarreling and killing. He was right, but his moral standards meant little to a different culture. The French had indulged the Indians in order to keep their friendship and increase the flow of furs. On top of the Indians' loss of gifts, the prices in furs that they had to pay the British for blankets, shirts, jewelry, knives, pans, and paint seemed high. Wherever French inhabitants remained, they supported the complaints of the Indians and spread rumors detrimental to the British.

Dissatisfaction with British rule was even greater among the Ottawa, Chippewa, Huron, and Potawatomi around Detroit.

Down in Ohio, a Delaware visionary, known only as the Delaware Prophet, was preaching a new gospel that the Indians, in order to survive, must throw off all white influence, beneficial as well as baneful, become completely self-sufficient as they had once been, and reclaim their land from white invaders. An Ottawa war chief named Pontiac from Detroit heard the Delaware Prophet and turned the spiritual message to his own ends: expulsion of the British and restoration of his French friends. He united the four villages on the Detroit River to attack the fort at Detroit. When his initial surprise failed, he began a siege and sent messengers to the other tribes in Ohio, Indiana, western Pennsylvania, and western New York to strike the British forts in their midst. He also dispatched an ambassadorial party of Ottawa and Frenchmen to Illinois to solicit aid from the French there. En route, that delegation aroused the Miami and the Wea. Ensign Holmes was called out of Fort Miamis by his Indian mistress in a ruse and was killed by a shot from ambush. His sergeant ran out to see what had happened and was seized by the Indians. The remainder of the garrison shut the gate, but on threat of being taken and killed, the soldiers agreed to surrender as prisoners. The couriers sent four of them back to Detroit to be paraded before Pontiac. The fate of the other ten men is not known.

Four days later, May 31, 1763, Pontiac's embassy reached Fort Ouiatenon and told the local tribes of the war against the English. They carried a belt of war wampum which the Wea, Kickapoo, and Mascouten accepted. They seized a few soldiers outside the fort and next morning called Lieutenant Jenkins to meet with their chiefs. As soon as he appeared, Jenkins was seized and bound and told to give up his men. He did so. The garrison was kept prisoner for two months, then taken to Fort de Chartres in Illinois, where the French commandant released them. By July, nine forts in the Great Lakes area had fallen to the Indians. Detroit was under siege, and so was Fort Pitt. British authority in Indiana no longer existed.

Early snow and a discouraging message from Illinois that the

French king had now made peace with the British king forced Pontiac to give up his siege of Detroit at the end of October 1763. The following summer, the British under General Thomas Gage mounted two expeditions to chastise the rebellious western tribes. Colonel Henry Bouquet, who had relieved Fort Pitt, was to march into the Ohio country, threaten the Shawnee and Delaware, take hostages for their good behavior, and recover white prisoners, all of which he accomplished. Another column under Colonel John Bradstreet coasted along Lake Erie on its way to Detroit. At the mouth of the Maumee, Bradstreet detached Captain Thomas Morris to go up the river and down the Wabash to Illinois. Eighteen miles upstream, however, at an Ottawa village, Morris came face to face with Pontiac, who was still belligerent. Nevertheless, Pontiac allowed Morris to proceed, and sent his nephew along as protector. Morris bought a volume of Shakespeare from an Indian for a little powder! Approaching Fort Miamis, Morris was greeted by the whole village of Kekionga in arms. The Miami stripped him of his clothes and bound him in one of their cabins. Two Kickapoo chiefs were visiting, and they warned Morris that, if he proceeded on to Fort Ouiatenon, they would kill him. Pontiac's nephew protested, and Morris's two French guides appealed to the young Miami chief, Pacanne, who called a council to deliberate. Their decision was that Morris could not go farther west, but if released must go overland at once to Detroit. Morris got his clothes back and departed. Arriving at Detroit, he reported to Bradstreet that the Indians west of that fort were still hostile.

Finally, in 1765, Indian agent George Croghan was sent to Illinois via the Ohio River to prepare the way for British occupation. He was accompanied by some white boatmen and several Shawnee, Delaware, and Seneca warriors who would testify that they had made peace with the British. At a campsite just beyond the mouth of the Wabash on June 7, Croghan's party was attacked by eighty Kickapoo and Mascouten, who killed five men, wounded all but three, and took the party prisoner.

"I got the Stroke of a hatchett on the Head," Croghan reported, ''but my Scull being pretty thick the hatchett wou'd not enter, so you may see a thick Scull is of Service on some Occasions.'' [2]

The prisoners were carried up to Vincennes. ''I found,'' Croghan wrote, and here his style is improved,

> a village of about 80 or 90 French families settled on the east side of the river, being one of the finest situations that can be found. The country is level and clear, and soil very rich, producing wheat and tobacco. . . . The French inhabitants hereabouts are an idle lazy people, a parcel of renegades from Canada, and are much worse than Indians. They took a secret pleasure at our misfortunes and the moment we arrived they came to the Indians, exchanging trifles for their valuable plunder. [3]

Only the local Piankashaw remonstrated with the captors for their foolish venture. Taken northward to Fort Ouiatenon, Croghan found about fourteen French families. ''The country hereabouts is exceedingly pleasant, being open and clear for many miles, the soil very rich and well watered.'' [4] It was here that Croghan met the elusive Pontiac, made peace with him, and gained his promise to go to Sir William Johnson, Crown Superintendent of Indian Affairs, in New York, and conclude formalities. Pontiac did make the journey to Johnson Hall in 1766, was treated with deference, and made his peace. Although shorn of power by his own people in consequence of his failure to force the British out, Pontiac lived with a few followers on an island in the Maumee. On a visit to Fort de Chartres in 1769, he was assassinated by another Indian, who was never caught.

The pre-Revolutionary turbulence in the thirteen English colonies was hardly felt in Indiana, and the war itself was ignored

2. Croghan to William Murray, July 12, 1765, Thomas Gage Papers, William L. Clements Library, University of Michigan, Ann Arbor, Mich.

3. Gayle Thornbrough and Dorothy L. Riker, ''George Croghan's Journal,'' in *Readings in Indiana History*, Indiana Historical Collections 36 (Indianapolis: Indiana Historical Bureau, 1956): 20, 22.

4. Thornbrough and Riker, ''George Croghan's Journal,'' p. 22.

for three years. Then young George Rogers Clark of Kentucky, a delegate to the Virginia House of Burgesses (Kentucky was a county of Virginia), appealed to Governor Patrick Henry to be allowed to protect the County of Kentucky by taking the offensive against British power in the West. It was the only way, Clark argued, to end the Indian raids inspired by the British. Governor Henry agreed with the tall, red-haired frontiersman, gave him a commission as lieutenant colonel, and provided some supplies. Clark raised 150 men in western Virginia and embarked them down the Ohio. He lost a few by desertion, but enlisted enough others in Kentucky to make his force 175. They marched across southern Illinois to the French settlement at Kaskaskia and took it without a shot on July 4, 1778. Able to tell the inhabitants of the alliance of France with the American colonies, Clark won their allegiance. Detachments sent to Cahokia and St. Genevieve met with equal success, as the French were glad to throw in with the Americans. The Illinois country was in rebel hands.

Clark dispatched the local priest, Father Pierre Gibault, and the local physician, Dr. Jean Laffont, along with a group of citizens to Vincennes. They were greeted warmly by the local inhabitants, who also took the oath of allegiance to Virginia. The absence of resistance permitted Captain Leonard Helm and three soldiers to serve as the new authority there. In Illinois, Clark was busy persuading the Indian tribes to support the "big knives," as they called Americans, or at least stay neutral.

Up at Detroit, the British commandant, Colonel Henry Hamilton, soon received the news of what had happened in his backyard. Further, Helm had got some reinforcements from Clark and rowed up the Wabash to Fort Ouiatenon to effect a treaty of friendship with the Wea and Kickapoo. Hamilton realized he must retaliate or face attack. He raised a force of 33 British regulars, 138 French and English militia, and—initially—70 Indians. Moving out slowly, he headed south and west, picking up new Indian allies. Some Miami joined him, but he was not impressed by the French. At Fort Miamis "a worthless set, deserters from Canada or Detroit," one officer recorded, with the Miami cabins "much preferable & Cleaner than the French." At Fort Ouiatenon were a dozen French cabins; adjacent were ninety cabins of the Wea, and farther down the river, ninety-six cabins of Kickapoo. Those tribes showed no compunction about switching back to British allegiance after Hamilton spoke to them.

The armed flotilla took an incredible seventy days to reach Vincennes, coming in sight of the town on December 17. Although the French militia had deserted, a pennant was still flying, and Captain Helm was able to demand the honors of war before surrendering the fort and becoming a prisoner. The Indians seized all the horses and almost everything else that was moveable. Hamilton found the fort a "miserable picketed work" and set his men to building barracks for themselves and two blockhouses for a few light cannon. The Indians left him, and most of the Detroit militia set off for home in January 1779.

It was the latter part of that month before Clark learned that Vincennes had been lost. Francis Vigo, a trader captured and released by Hamilton, reported in detail on British strength. Clark did not hesitate; he knew he must act first, before Hamilton obtained reinforcements and advanced on the Illinois settlements. Although he could raise only 210 men, half of them French volunteers, Clark wrote to Governor Patrick Henry that "great things have been effected by a few Men well Conducted; perhaps we may be fortunate." [5] He sent a boatload of provisions with 40 men aboard by way of the Mississippi, the Ohio, and the Wabash. With 170 men, Clark set off overland on a march of 180 miles in February. An early thaw melted snow and ice, flooding lowlands and forcing the soldiers to do much slow wading. Near the Wabash, tributary streams flooded an area almost five miles wide. Finding patches of dry land and crossing the Wabash with a shuttle of two canoes, the cold, hungry, and exhausted troops came in sight of Vincennes on February 22. Clark sent a brusque message to the French inhabi-

5. Clark to Patrick Henry, February 3, 1779, Indiana Historical Society Library, Indianapolis, Ind.

tants to stay in their houses or join the British within the fort. He then paraded his men in such a fashion and at such a distance that observers would estimate his force at a thousand. That night he started firing on the fort. Next day Hamilton asked for terms. Clark was tough. During negotiations, a party of Indians returned from a raid into Kentucky, and the Americans tomahawked four of them in full view of the fort. Hamilton surrendered his garrison of 79, of whom 33 were regulars. He and the latter were sent as prisoners of war to Williamsburg, Virginia. The French swore American allegiance again, and Clark let the remaining French militia return to Detroit. A convoy of British provisions coming down the Wabash was seized, and Clark's own boat reached Vincennes. The town was incorporated into the huge County of Illinois, created by Virginia.

Full of hope and determination, Clark expected to march on Detroit in the summer of 1779, but Virginia sent only 150 men to him, and Kentucky diverted its reinforcement to a raid on the Shawnee town of Chillicothe in Ohio. Reluctantly, Clark gave up his attempt, put Captain James Shelby in command at Vincennes, and returned to Louisville. The next year, troops were removed from Vincennes, but the British made no further attempt against it.

A French officer, Augustin de la Balme, who had come to America with Lafayette, appeared in Illinois and later at Vincennes, in 1780, to undertake an expedition against Detroit. He could not raise a hundred men. He detached sixteen of them from Cahokia to capture Fort St. Joseph (Niles, Michigan), a successful mission, but on their return they were overtaken near modern Tremont, Indiana, and severely defeated. La Balme led about eighty men up the Wabash and easily captured Fort Miamis, but the Indians turned against him and he was killed, along with many of his troops.

Another flicker of the Revolution occurred in Indiana early in 1781, when a detachment of Spaniards from St. Louis (Spain was, at the time, an ally of the Americans) attacked Fort St. Joseph again, captured a few British traders, raised a Spanish flag, and promptly departed back across northwestern Indiana.

The last conflict on Hoosier soil occurred in August 1781. Still hoping to strike Detroit, Clark was waiting in Kentucky for reinforcements from Pennsylvania. Colonel Archibald Lochry, bringing a pitiful force of 107 men down the Ohio to join Clark, camped at the mouth of Laughery Creek in Dearborn County on August 24. The noted Mohawk, Captain Joseph Brant, with a force of Canadians and Indians, surprised and killed about a third of the Pennsylvanians, capturing the rest. Most of the prisoners, including Lochry, were butchered later. There would still be savage battles in Kentucky, but Indiana was spared further bloodshed.

Clark's partial conquest of the Northwest was known to the peacemakers in Paris. How decisive it was is still argued. Apparently it strengthened the American claim to the region, and Spain's effort to claim it was rejected by the British negotiators. The present boundary through the Great Lakes was agreed upon, and it is only speculation to say it would have been, anyway, without George Rogers Clark's astonishing success.

A grateful Virginia, at least, granted Clark's men 150,000 acres of land on the north side of the Ohio. The spot selected was opposite the Falls of the Ohio at Louisville. The town site was named Clarksville, and it still stands in Indiana. Clark's cousin, William Clark, was appointed principal surveyor, and settlement began in 1784, four years before Marietta, far up the river, was founded and frequently called the first American settlement in the Northwest Territory. Clark himself established a residence in the town and built a sawmill and a gristmill. He was followed by twenty or thirty other settlers, with families. Clark's men who took up the plots allotted to them were largely from Virginia and Pennsylvania. When Virginia surrendered her western claims to the Continental Congress, Clark's grant was specifically exempted.

Conditions at Vincennes were far from happy. Its government had been neglected by Virginia, and relations between the few civil authorities, the military, and the French were unpleasant. When John Finley, Kentucky's first historian, visited the place in 1785, he found it contained about three hundred houses, "most of which make a poor appearance." In contrast to earlier reports, he characterized the French as "perhaps no people in the world more friendly and cleanly," and "a people naturally obedient to authority," although numbers of them "live as savages in some respects and many are intermarried with them." [6] Perhaps seventy Americans, as individuals or families, had moved in, probably from Kentucky, and were either squatters or owners of land granted to them by dishonest officials.

Congress stationed the tiny standing army of the United States (one regiment) on the Ohio River to protect both surveyors and settlers against Indians who felt that Great Britain had no right to give away their land to the new United States of America. The colonel-commandant, Josiah Harmar, made a military tour in 1787 to Vincennes and Illinois. He reported that Vincennes contained about nine hundred French and four hundred Americans. Almost all the latter were farmers. He left Major John F. Hamtramck and a garrison of ninety-five troops; their first job was to build a new fort, which they located outside the village and named Fort Knox, for U.S. Secretary of War Henry Knox. Fluent in French and Catholic in religious belief, Hamtramck resolved most of the difficulties with the French, Americans, and Indians and remained in command for seven years. To settle the confused state of land titles in the community, Congress in 1791 allowed four hundred acres to every French family, with another hundred acres if a member had served in the militia. However, many of the French sold their lands to the Americans because they did not want to farm and reverted to their small gardens and hunting and trapping.

The land ordinance of 1785 had defined the manner of surveying the Northwest Territory so as to insure clear titles and the selling of tracts to settlers. Another ordinance, passed by Congress in 1787, created the Northwest Territory, provided for its immediate government, and set procedures for creation of subsequent states to join the Union. Precepts set forth in that Northwest Ordinance have been followed as recently as in the admission of Alaska and Hawaii. It set the number of states to be formed from the Northwest Territory at no fewer than three,

6. *Mississippi Valley Historical Review* 9, 326–327.

no more than five; specified the steps that the residents of those areas must follow to qualify for statehood; guaranteed several civil rights, prohibited slavery, and required that sales revenue from part of the public lands be used to support public schools. Congress appointed Arthur St. Clair, a major general of the Revolution, as the territory's first governor. Indiana Territory, established in 1800 in anticipation of Ohio's entering the Union, included the rest of the old Northwest Territory, but it was subsequently reduced in size by formation of Michigan, Illinois, and Wisconsin territories. Indiana became a state in 1816, Illinois in 1818, Michigan in 1837, and Wisconsin in 1848. It was the Northwest Ordinance, as much as the rich land and minerals in the area, that stimulated immigration, and its provisions solved the problem of embracing colonies into a nation—a political issue that had baffled the British empire.

Only the Indian problem was left unresolved. Were the tribes sovereign nations with full title to the land over which they hunted? Were they merely occupants who could be forced to sell out? Were they children of nature who should be taught farming in order to raise their living standard and incidentally reduce the vast hunting area they currently needed? Were they primitive savages who, like the wolves of the forest, must be driven out or exterminated before advancing Christians of a higher culture? All these attitudes were adopted by various groups of Americans and revealed a congeries of arrogance, sympathy, hostility, generosity, vindictiveness, and evangelism. Whichever diagnosis the U.S. government made, the Indians would not accept it. Out of a different culture, they subscribed to different values. The two races met and counseled, but spoke on two different levels. Neither could satisfy the other.

Roiling the water in the Old Northwest, the defeated British hung on to Niagara, Detroit, and Mackinac Island, and the United States literally had no one in the area to assume control of those posts, which were rich fur-trading depots. In addition, the British were not averse to encouraging the Indians to slow the advancing Americans. As a result of raids on new settlements, General Harmar in 1790 was ordered to undertake an expedition against the Miami on the headwaters of the Maumee. Harmar left Fort Washington (Cincinnati) with 320 regulars and 1,133 militia from Kentucky, Virginia, and Pennsylvania. There was no time to train the militia before starting the northward march. At their destination, they found the Miami towns deserted. Harmar burned the towns and surrounding fields. He sent out a detachment of 210 men under Colonel John Hardin of Kentucky to look for the fugitives. Down the St. Joseph River, Hardin found them—in an ambush. Hardin lost 20 regulars and 40 militia before many of the latter fled. He felt disgraced, and after Harmar started his expedition toward home, Hardin asked to go back and surprise any returning Miami and redeem his Kentucky troops. Reluctantly, Harmar acquiesced and allowed him 300 militia and 60 regulars under Major John P. Willys. It was a repeat performance: at first the Indians fled, and the militia broke ranks and scattered in pursuit. Another body of Indians then came out of hiding and overwhelmed the regulars, killing 50 of them and the major, as well. In the disaster, more than 100 were wounded. A chastened Hardin rejoined Harmar, and the reduced expedition hurried back to Fort Washington. The Indians felt elated and ready for further offensives.

Three hundred other militia had been forwarded to Major Hamtramck, and in a co-ordinated move he was to march up the Wabash and strike the Wea and Kickapoo. He too found deserted villages, which he burned. He had already suffered some desertions on the eleven-day tramp, and since he lacked enough provisions to go on another week to old Fort Ouiatenon, Hamtramck gave up and returned to Vincennes. Had he kept on, he would have encountered 600 warriors up the Wabash who probably would have treated him as Hardin had been treated.

Virginia reacted first to the defeat by authorizing Brigadier General Charles Scott of Kentucky to enlist mounted volunteers. The force was then offered to Secretary of War Knox, who directed Scott to wipe out the Wea village. With 800 armed men, Scott rode right up through the future Indiana in May 1791. He had Colonel Hardin with him, and this time Hardin performed better. He was sent off to the left to attack the Kickapoo, while Scott advanced to the Wabash and fired into a Wea village. The river could not be forded there, so Scott divided his force, one wing crossing upstream and the other crossing downstream. Hardin drove out the Kickapoo, killing 6 and capturing 52 women and children. That night Colonel James Wilkinson took 360 men and rode eighteen miles north to the Wea town of Kathtippecamunk, near the mouth of the Tippecanoe River. When he arrived, at dawn, the Indians were leaving. Several were killed in a brisk fire, and the town of some seventy cabins was burned, along with a quantity of corn and fur pelts. Scott's force carried prisoners back to Kentucky, having lost only two men killed and two wounded.

The success of this expedition prompted a second stroke by Wilkinson and 500 Kentucky mounted volunteers in August. They rode straight north from Fort Washington as if headed for the Miami on the Maumee, but suddenly turned west to a Miami village called Kenapacomaqua, where Chief Little Turtle lived, on the Wabash at the mouth of the Eel River. Wilkinson completely surprised the town, but had to attack at dusk. He killed 11 warriors, captured 40 women and children, and burned all the huts and 200 acres of corn. He returned by way of the sacked Wea town and burned the new crop of corn.

Both of these enterprises were minor victories, and a major expedition was organized to avenge Harmar's mauling. This time the governor of the Northwest Territory, Major General Arthur St. Clair, himself, would lead it. Fort Washington again was the rendezvous for the promised 3,000 troops. St. Clair was to build a chain of forts northward and then construct a large one at the head of the Maumee, so as to keep the Miami in order. The militia, due by July 1, did not arrive until September and then numbered fewer than expected. St. Clair moved out on September 17, 1791, and built Fort Hamilton and Fort Jefferson, both of which had to be garrisoned. The term for which some of the soldiers had enlisted expired, and they would not proceed; others began to desert. Foolishly, St. Clair sent his best regulars to chase the deserters, while he marched the remainder of his army to the headwaters of the Wabash. He went into camp on November 3 with 1,400 men. Early the next morning, about a thousand Indians of several tribes under Little Turtle struck suddenly. The militia fled, the guns were abandoned, the regulars were no match for the attackers, and soon the whole army was in retreat. The killed and wounded amounted to 928, the worst defeat suffered by American arms up to modern times. Migration into the West was checked. President Washington was angry and chagrined. He appointed his old comrade Anthony Wayne to command the U.S. Army and to reorganize it.

At the same time, the government tried to negotiate a peace with the Indians, but the British were advising the red men to resist. General Wayne began collecting and training recruits at Fort Pitt. In 1793 he established his headquarters at Fort Washington and continued his training camp. In the fall he moved northward and established Fort Greenville, above Fort Jefferson, where he spent the winter. Early in 1794 he moved to the scene of St. Clair's defeat and erected a post called Fort Recovery. The Indians could see what was coming and attacked the post without success. Little Turtle then advised his fellow chiefs to negotiate, but they would not listen. The lieutenant governor of Upper Canada, John Graves Simcoe, urged Indian resistance and even built a fort at the Maumee rapids—on U.S. soil! In London, John Jay was trying to unravel this knot with an empire involved in war with France.

Wayne advanced to the Maumee River at the mouth of the Auglaize, where he built Fort Defiance. He offered a treaty of peace to the Indians, but they rejected it unless the Americans would pull their settlements back to the Ohio River. In August Wayne turned eastward, down the river, toward the illegal British fort. With a reinforcement of mounted volunteers from Kentucky, he had about 3,000 troops. Within two miles of the place, he came upon a wooded area in which a tornado had touched down, uprooting trees that formed natural breastworks. Here the Indians, under the Shawnee chief Blue Jacket, had decided to make a stand. Some 1,500 Miami, Shawnee, Delaware, Ottawa, Huron, and possibly some Wea, Potawatomi, and Kickapoo, along with perhaps 500 whites from Detroit, took up concealed positions across the line of march. They were provisioned by the British.

Wayne was not surprised. On the morning of August 20, 1794, he formed his troops for the Battle of Fallen Timbers, sending the mounted riflemen in a sweep to outflank the Indians, while his disciplined infantry stormed through the underbrush of fallen trees. Such audacity tested the Indians severely. They fought for three hours before breaking in retreat. They ran back to the fort for protection and got the surprise of their lives. The British refused to open the gates and let them in. Howling in frustration, they fled on down the river bank. Wayne marched up to the fort and exchanged insults with the commandant, while laying waste the cornfields, the storehouse, and the residence of the British Indian agent. With unaccustomed caution, he avoided starting a war with England before turning back west.

At the head of the Maumee, near Kekionga, Wayne began a large new fort. Colonel Hamtramck was called from Vincennes to be commandant of what he named Fort Wayne. The garrison was made up of five companies of infantry and one of artillery. The U.S. Army was there to stay. Wayne took his remaining force back to Fort Greenville and prepared for a great council with the Indians, anticipating that they would now come to him and sue for peace.

In November the London government concluded a treaty with John Jay and agreed to withdraw all British troops and garrisons from within the boundary lines determined in 1783. Thus both the arrogant Canadian officials and the Indian chiefs learned there would be no English support to challenges of United States jurisdiction over the Northwest. If the chiefs were bitter, they knew what they had to do. Delay and demands for compensation were their only weapons against the Americans. They gathered slowly at Greenville, the representatives of a dozen tribes, and made preparations for peace. They acknowledged that white settlement could proceed in about two-thirds of the future state of Ohio and a small triangle of future southeastern Indiana called the "gore." In addition, certain sites and portages, such as Fort Wayne, Ouiatenon, Vincennes, and Clark's Grant, were ceded to the United States. In return, the Indians received goods valued at $20,000 and annual payments of goods valued at $9,500. The treaty was signed on August 3, 1795. Plans were made by Wayne to move his troops the next summer to take over Detroit and Mackinac Island.

What would peace bring? Immigration resumed into modern Ohio, but not into Indiana. Clark's Grant did not attract all the soldiers entitled to land. No new community besides Clarksville materialized in Indiana, although squatters from Kentucky did cross the river and settle individually in southern Indiana. Constantin Volney, French historian and traveler, visited Vincennes in 1796 and attended a court session:

> As soon as I entered I was struck at seeing the audience divided into two races of men, totally different in features and in person. One had a fair or light brown hair, ruddy complexions, full faces, and a plumpness of body that announced health and ease; the other, very meager countenances, a sallow tawny skin, and the whole body as if emaciated with fasting, not to speak of their clothes, which sufficiently denoted their poverty. I presently discovered that the latter were the French settlers, who had been about sixty years in the place; while the former were Americans, who cultivated the land they had bought only five or six years before.[7]

Enough people were in the eastern part of the Northwest Territory to force reluctant Governor Arthur St. Clair to proclaim the area ready in 1798 for the second stage of government as provided in the Ordinance of 1787. Elections for twenty-two members of a lower house of assembly were held, and John Small was chosen a member from Knox County, which lay in the future Indiana. When the assembly met and submitted ten names to President John Adams for a legislative council of five, one of the appointees was Henry Vanderburgh of Vincennes. The full assembly met in Cincinnati in 1799 and elected, as the

---

7. C. F. Volney, *A View of the Soil and Climate of the United States of America* . . . (Philadelphia: J. Conrad and Co., 1804), p. 369.

first delegate to Congress from the Northwest Territory, William Henry Harrison, who had served under Anthony Wayne.

Indiana Territory was set off in 1800, as the area east of it prepared to enter the Union as the state of Ohio. In consequence, the new Indiana Territory reverted to the first stage of territorial government, that by an appointed governor, secretary, and three judges. During his one year in Congress, Harrison had made a name for himself as proponent of an act to allow purchases in the Northwest of fewer than 640 acres (a square mile). Settlers could now buy half that amount, pay down only a quarter of the price (two dollars an acre), and take four years to pay the remainder in annual installments. President Adams appointed the twenty-seven-year-old Harrison as governor of Indiana Territory, with the capital at Vincennes. The secretary was John Gibson of Pennsylvania, whose wife was a sister of Shawnee Chief Logan, and the three judges named were Henry Vanderburgh of Vincennes; William Clarke, a U.S. attorney then serving in Kentucky; and John Griffin of Virginia.

The census of 1800 indicated about 2,500 people within what is now Indiana. Clark's Grant contained 929. The "gore" of southeastern Indiana may have harbored as many squatters. Fort Wayne held perhaps 40 or 50, besides the garrison. Vincennes counted 714 in the town and 819 in the neighborhood, but many of the latter in all probability were across the river in modern Illinois. There may have been a dozen Frenchmen still at Ouiatenon.

Despite his political experience and his familiarity with the arbitrary acts of Governor St. Clair as a caution, Harrison soon found it impossible to please everyone. The scion of a famous Virginia family, he first tried a medical career and then obtained a commission in the army in 1791. Wayne found him courageous, conscientious, and intelligent, and made him his aide. Harrison had married the daughter of Judge John Cleves Symmes of Cincinnati in 1795; he resigned from the army three years later.

As governor, Harrison's appointments and policies drew the more conservative men in the territory to his side and antago-

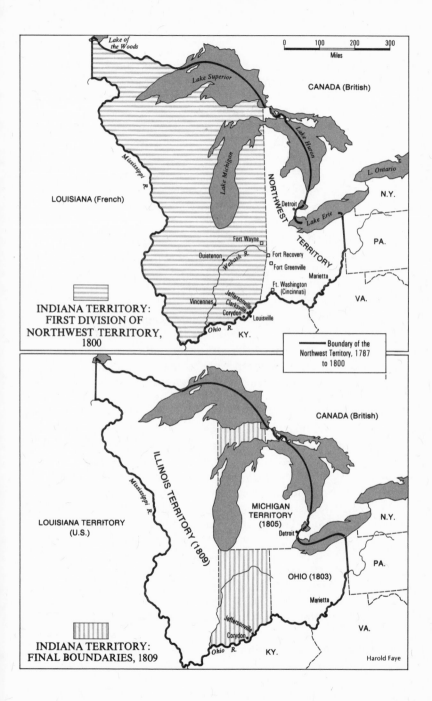

Lake of
the Woods

Lake Superior

CANADA (British)

Lake Huron

Mississippi R.

Lake Michigan

NORTHWEST

L. Ontario

N.Y.

Detroit

Lake Erie

PA.

LOUISIANA (French)

TERRITORY

Fort Wayne

Ouiatenon

Wabash R.

Fort Recovery

Fort Greenville

Marietta

VA.

Ft. Washington
(Cincinnati)

Jeffersonville

Vincennes

Clarksville

Corydon

Louisville

Ohio R.

KY.

INDIANA TERRITORY:
FIRST DIVISION OF
NORTHWEST TERRITORY,
1800

Boundary of the
Northwest Territory, 1787
to 1800

CANADA (British)

ILLINOIS TERRITORY (1809)

Mississippi R.

MICHIGAN
TERRITORY
(1805)

N.Y.

Detroit

LOUISIANA TERRITORY
(U.S.)

OHIO (1803)

PA.

Marietta

Jeffersonville

VA.

Corydon

Ohio R.

KY.

Harold Faye

INDIANA TERRITORY:
FINAL BOUNDARIES, 1809

nized ambitious young men and new settlers. Imbued with a sense of equality, many people felt that the government should be responsive to their wishes, even though it had not been elected by them. In fact, their main desire was to win control of it by achieving statehood as quickly as possible, as the total population began to rise toward the qualifying figure of 5,000 adult males. Although Harrison had made his career in the Northwest, it was easy to characterize him as a Virginia aristocrat, especially after he built an imposing two-story brick house in Vincennes not unlike his father's home on the James River. Further, he was not opposed to slavery.

Harrison created a second Indiana county named Clark, out of the eastern half of Knox County, and appointed judges and other local officials for it. Attempting to insure justice to the Indians, he issued a proclamation forbidding whites from settling or hunting on any of the Indian lands and prohibiting the sale of liquor to Indians within a mile of Vincennes. He also contributed further to his Virginia image by falling under the sway of petitioners who wanted the antislavery article of the Ordinance of 1787 repealed. Harrison went so far as to call for an election of twelve delegates to meet in December 1802 at Vincennes to discuss possible changes in the Northwest Ordinance. This body passed a resolution in favor of a ten-year suspension of Article VI of the Ordinance, on the ground that Indiana would attract more settlers if they could bring their slaves with them. The proposal was buried among other proposed changes in the Ordinance to which Congress paid no attention. So in 1803 the governor and the judges, in their legislative capacity, adopted a Virginia law permitting lifetime contracts between masters and servants. Thus slavery continued among a select few in Indiana Territory, to the annoyance of the majority.

In 1804 Elihu Stout established in Vincennes a newspaper, which had the effect of spotlighting politics and allowing opinions to be publicized. It encouraged the development of proslavery and antislavery factions as well as parties—Federalists and Democratic Republicans. The geographical focus of contention narrowed as Michigan Territory was set off in 1805, and Illinois Territory in 1809, leaving Indiana reduced to its present size.

Towns were being founded in this decade along the Ohio–Lawrenceburg, Jeffersonville, Madison, Charlestown, Aurora. An unexpected accretion occurred when 2,500 French-speaking Swiss settled in 1801 on a spot they named Vevay, for their home town, with the purpose of cultivating grape vines and making wine. In 1805 Andrew McFadden opened a post—renamed Mount Vernon—in the toe of the boot. On the Buffalo Trace from Clarksville to Vincennes, Fredericksburg was established. Up the Whitewater River, a party of South Carolinians founded Fairfield, some North Carolina Quakers settled Richmond, and then Brookville appeared in 1808. Corydon, west of Clarksville, was established the same year, and John Conner set up his trading post at the future Connersville. The census of 1810 showed 24,500 people in four counties.

Governor Harrison found that much of his time had to be given over to treating with irreconcilable Indian leaders. The chiefs, who had denied in 1763 the right of France to do more than transfer her scattered forts in the Great Lakes region to England, were supplanted by chiefs who denied the right of England in 1783 to do more than transfer those same posts to the United States. In 1795 those chiefs who agreed to settlements in Ohio comprehended that that was the penalty of defeat by the Americans and desertion by the British. Indiana, in their view, remained Indian territory, however, except for the three forts and Clark's Grant. Yet settlers were steadily creeping north from the Ohio River. Harrison had an impossible task to justify the intrusion to the Indians; he could only hope to buy the land from them.

His first council, in 1802, brought 500 Indians, including women and children, to Vincennes. Its simple purpose was to define the tract of land along the Wabash, above and below Vincennes, which the French claimed the Indians had ceded to them in 1742 and which was recognized in the Treaty of Greenville. The chiefs agreed to relinquish a long, irregular rectangle of land on both sides of the river from its mouth northward for thirty-seven miles. President Jefferson wrote to Harrison early in 1803 his naive faith that "the decrease of game rendering their subsistence by hunting insufficient, we wish to draw them to agriculture, to spinning & weaving.'' He also believed they would be willing to offer land ''from time to time in exchange for necessaries for their farms & families.''

In August 1804 Harrison met the Delaware chiefs and bought the right of white settlement in the tract south of the Buffalo Trace (Clarksville to Vincennes). The overlapping claim of the Piankashaw was also relinquished for a price. When some Miami objected, Harrison invited them, along with the Potawatomi, Wea, and Delaware, to a council in 1805. By disbursing $4,000 and increasing annuities, he obtained title to some of southeastern Indiana extending to the Ohio line. The lower fourth of the future state was now cleared of Indian title, and Harrison declared the Territory ready for its second stage of government: the election on January 3, 1805, of nine representatives to govern the area along with an appointed council or upper house.

A new tribe now occupied Harrison's attention. The Shawnee, dispossessed in Ohio by settlements following the Treaty of Greenville in 1795, came into northern Indiana as refugees. They produced two leaders of considerable influence—Tecumseh and his one-eyed brother, Tenskwatawa, better known as the Shawnee Prophet. Tecumseh was a political organizer and diplomat, his brother a moral leader and orator. Both were in their forties at this time. Neither had any military acumen. The Shawnee Prophet took up an old line from the Delaware Prophet, who had influenced Pontiac in 1762, preaching separation from the whites and all their culture, advocating teetotalism, truth-telling, and a return to Indian methods and customs. He was well received among the Delaware of White River and in 1807 called an assembly of all the Northwest tribes at Greenville for a kind of religious revival, yet inevitably poised against U.S. policy. Nothing came of it, but the next year the Prophet established a Shawnee village on the Wabash near the mouth of the Tippecanoe River, above modern Lafayette.

In an effort to open more of Indiana to settlement, Harrison journeyed to Fort Wayne in 1809 and in a concourse of nearly 1,400 Indians (Miami, Wea, Potawatomi, Delaware), he bought two large tracts in eastern and western parts of the state, almost three million acres altogether. The Shawnee Prophet decried the treaty and declared no sale was valid unless all tribes agreed. Tecumseh now assumed an active role. He called on Harrison at Vincennes in August 1810 and grew threatening against both the chiefs who had signed the previous year's treaty and the Americans. Nothing was accomplished. Tecumseh returned in July 1811 with a large retinue and denied Harrison's accusations that he was inciting the Indians against the U.S. government. He insisted his aim was peace, that no hostilities would be committed, and that he was going south to unite all the tribes in a peaceful league. Harrison did not believe him and suggested to the secretary of war that Tecumseh's "absence affords a most favorable opportunity for breaking up his Confederacy." The secretary agreed; he had already sent the U.S. Fourth Regiment to Kentucky, and he placed it under Harrison's orders.

The governor was intent on making a demonstration of force by marching up the Wabash to the farthest point of the 1809 purchase, which would bring him close to the Shawnee Prophet's town. He put 350 regulars from the Fourth Regiment and 650 militia in motion on September 26. Near modern Terre Haute, the expedition halted for a month and built a fort, named for Harrison. During that interval, John Tipton, a volunteer who later became a U.S. senator from Indiana, recorded meeting a Delaware chief who spoke good English and liked to play cards with the soldiers. The Miami, Wea, and part of the Potawatomi were reported to be deserting the Prophet. The march was now resumed, and on November 6 the army turned north of the Wabash and approached the Shawnee town from the west. Some chiefs came out to meet it and asked for a council on the morrow. Harrison agreed and went into camp. Before dawn, the Shawnee attacked. The troops, sleeping on their arms, rallied at once and formed around the camp. The dark battle lasted for two hours, until daylight appeared, then the Indians withdrew. Harrison suffered 200 casualties. The attackers, who, Harrison believed, numbered almost 700, left 35 to 40 dead on the field, and additional bodies were found in the deserted town, which the army burned. Thirty years after it had taken place, the Battle of Tippecanoe helped make Harrison president. Today, a tall shaft marks the battle site, seven miles north of Lafayette.

This curtain raiser for the War of 1812 bred retaliatory raids and pushed some of the Northwest tribes into active co-operation again with the British. The clock was set back twenty years. On September 3 a war party of Shawnee and Delaware penetrated as far south as the hamlet of Pigeon Roost, in Scott County, less than twenty miles from the Ohio River, and killed twenty-four men, women, and children and burned six houses. A week earlier, other Indians—Potawatomi and Miami—laid siege to Fort Wayne, and a drunken commandant offered no resistance. Harrison had gone to Kentucky hoping to receive a general's commission and had accepted command of the Kentucky militia while waiting. He began marching toward the relief of Detroit, but learning that it had fallen, he turned aside and relieved Fort Wayne of its siege on September 10. He then destroyed all the Indian villages in the vicinity. Late in the month, he received word that he was to command the Northwestern Army. His duties as governor were taken over by Thomas Posey, a Virginia veteran of the Revolution who was U.S. senator from Louisiana when appointed.

Indiana's taste of war did not end. Late in 1812, another future president, Captain Zachary Taylor, who had held Fort Harrison against Indian attack in September, marched up the Wabash and laid waste three Indian towns. In December Harrison sent Colonel John B. Campbell from Ohio with six hundred men to strike the Miami villages on the Mississinewa. Following their usual stratagem, the Indians fled ahead of him, but recoiled to assault the army camp early in the morning. Campbell lost eight killed and forty-two wounded in repulsing the attack. About half of his force was frostbitten, and they returned slowly to Ohio.

During 1813 individual families suffered destruction or death from Indian war parties, and local militia retaliated by burning Indian villages. In general, the Indians either followed Tecumseh into Canada or pulled back northward to avoid Hoosier raids. Detroit was recovered, and Tecumseh was killed in battle on the Thames River in Ontario. A big council was held at Greenville again, and Harrison once more offered peace if the Indians would join the Americans against the British when needed. The Indians agreed, but their aid was never requested. The war moved out of the Northwest and was ended early in 1815. Defeat of the Indians in Indiana and the rise of a new spirit of nationalism were the most important results of the conflict for the incipient state.

As part of the opposition to Harrison's friends left in Vincennes, the assembly moved the capital southeastward to the little town of Corydon in 1813, where a pleasant stone capitol was erected. Restored, it still stands. The once-large four counties were subdivided to make ten, and the lower house of the legislature was reapportioned. Three more counties were created in 1814, so that all of Indiana fronting on the Ohio River was organized into two layers of counties.

Cessation of hostilities and reduction of the Indian threat opened the floodgates of immigration. Not only did new settlers push up the Whitewater and the Wabash; they also came up the two forks of White River (which empties into the Wabash) and overland northward from the Ohio River ports. There were problems in providing enough courts and judges and jails, but no matter; the lure of the land remained. The territory took its own census in 1815, through tax collectors, and found 64,000 inhabitants, more than enough for statehood.

In December 1815 the legislators petitioned Congress for an election to choose delegates for a constitutional convention. Governor Posey objected to that move, partly because his appointive term was expiring and he wanted another term, and partly because he felt the settlers were not prosperous enough to support a state government and not widely educated enough to provide men of talent to fill the state offices. Wrong as he was, it is an interesting commentary. In contrast, William Hendricks of Madison, co-publisher of the *Western Eagle,* declared in a mixed metaphor that "no country ever presented more candidates for its population than does Indiana, to lay the foundation of our proposed State fabrick." [8] Congress passed an enabling act on April 19, 1816, and a constitutional convention of forty-three delegates met in June 1816 in Corydon. Jonathan Jennings, politically ambitious newcomer, was elected president. Born in the East in 1784, Jennings grew up in Pennsylvania and migrated to Vincennes in 1807 to seek fame and fortune. He was admitted to practice law and at once set himself in opposition to Governor Harrison politically. The next year, he found it prudent to move eastward into Clark County for greater opportunity. In April 1809 he was elected territorial delegate to Congress as an antislavery and anti-Harrison candidate. He had won re-election, too, but returned from Washington with his eye on a larger plum.

William Hendricks, who was not a delegate, was named secretary of the convention. More than half the delegates had some legal training or experience. Eight were militia officers, and four were ministers. Twenty-five of them might be classified as Southerners in origin, although the one born in South Carolina was the most vehement antislavery spokesman. James Dill, from Dearborn County, son-in-law of Governor Arthur St. Clair, and a loyal friend of Harrison, wrote: "The truth is Talents are most damnably lacking here—and he who has but a moderate share is looked upon as a great man." [9] John Badollet, a native of Switzerland who had lived in Pennsylvania before migrating to Vincennes, agreed. He found "several thinking men" in the convention, but the majority were "empty babblers, democratic to madness, having incessantly the *people* in their mouths and their dear selves in their eyes." [10]

Nevertheless, the delegates resolved themselves into committees that worked on various sections of the constitution, using the charters of Ohio and Kentucky principally as models. They

8. *Indiana Magazine of History* 39, 1943: 291.

9. John D. Barnhart and Dorothy L. Riker, *Indiana to 1816, the Colonial Period* (Indianapolis: Indiana Historical Society, 1971), p. 446.

10. *Correspondence of John Badollet and Albert Gallatin, 1804–1836*, edited by Gayle Thornbrough (Indianpolis: Indiana Historical Society, 1963), p. 263.

were concerned with democratic principles, making many offices elective and short-termed, and slavery was outlawed. An acceptable document was ready on June 29 and became operative without a ratification vote by the people. Elections were held in August, and the new state government began early in November. Jonathan Jennings was chosen the first state governor, which he had yearned to be. Indiana was formally admitted to the Union in December 1816 as the nineteenth state.

The new Hoosiers should have been exhausted. Collectively, they had been through two wars, two periods of Indian hostility, and two forms of government. Yet there was a resilience and enthusiasm about them that could not be stifled. A post-Revolutionary generation of varied origin, they were now committed to a common peacetime endeavor. The last Indian resistance and foreign war which had united them most recently was finished. Indians were still about, of course, but they had little political and economic influence, which was also true of the few Negroes in the new state. But the dominant whites in Indiana would have to learn to get along together if they were to govern themselves. That was part of what their pioneering had achieved: the chance to develop a distinctive, workable state.

3

Hoosiers Find Themselves

*T*HE new state aroused new ambitions and attracted new immigration. "Movers" from North Carolina, Virginia, and Kentucky poured across the Ohio, and others from Pennsylvania, New Jersey, and New York floated down the river from Pittsburgh. They were ready and eager to expand and shape the new commonwealth. The prospect was exciting. It was a free state, and there were no property qualifications for citizen voting. How would it develop?

In the first forty years of statehood, Hoosiers were sanguine, yet uncertain of the direction they wanted to take. Freedom to manage their own affairs, after sixteen years of appointed officials and outside threats, was exhilarating, but sign posts were missing. Consequently, they would try more than one life style, entertain various expressions of Christian faith, go at education backwards, rush disastrously into internal improvements, pursue inconsistent racial policies, join new political parties, move their capital, rewrite their state constitution, and argue vehemently about extinguishing slavery in the nation. But nothing dimmed their faith in the perfectibility of mankind or in themselves. They would prevail. Trials and errors obscured an emerging design, but the realistic pattern was clear and stable by 1860.

Southerners swarmed in first, and for a time the rest of the country wondered if Indiana might become a northern salient of the South, although the climate was such that it could be neither a cotton nor a tobacco state. Indiana became unique as a cross-current in the general westward tide across the continent: here the movement of settlement was from south to north. Eventually, Southerners reached the Wabash River and occasionally crossed it. Regardless of their adherence to Southern folkways, however, the Southern settlers in Indiana did not like slavery. They felt it was morally wrong, and some of them had found it economically destructive of their ambitions to get ahead on their own. Planter-dominated politics had further alienated them.

Tom Lincoln was probably typical of those who came in from Kentucky. Because the state had never been surveyed under the scientific system adopted for the Northwest Territory, and its land records were not well kept, boundaries were still defined in terms of trees and stones and brush piles and other impermanent markers, instead of lines of longitude and latitude. Deeds were not always recorded where they should be. Disputes were common, and overlapping or previously unknown claims caused men to lose land they had improved. Tom Lincoln had suffered that trouble with two farms in Kentucky, so he struck out for Indiana in 1816 to start over with a solid claim irrefutably his own. He also wanted to get out of a slave state.

After buying 160 acres on Little Pigeon Creek in old Perry (now Spencer) County, about sixteen miles above the Ohio River, he moved his family northward in December 1816. He had been married ten years and, besides his wife Nancy, had a daughter Sarah, aged nine, and a son Abraham, aged seven. Both children had gone to school in Kentucky, and the precocious boy could both read and write. The family brought along four horses, a cow, a wagon loaded with a spinning wheel, various farm implements, Tom's carpentry tools, and Nancy's utensils and bedding, and here they would stay for fourteen years, Tom farming and doing carpentry work. After a few days in a half-faced camp, Tom raised a log cabin and began making furniture, perhaps with his son's help. Then there were fields to be cleared, endless ax work and burning, before extensive crops could be planted. He paid down eighty dollars, or a quarter of the price, for his land.

As schooling was unavailable, Nancy encouraged her children's reading. In the fall of 1818, however, two years after they had come to Indiana, she died of the mysterious "milk-sick," contracted from the cow that had fed on the poisonous snakeroot. Tom and Abe made her coffin and buried her, a few hundred feet from the cabin. Sarah, almost twelve, became the housekeeper, but fourteen months later Tom Lincoln returned to Kentucky, seeking a wife. He married a widow, Sally Bush Johnston, with three children. She brought good furniture, books, and a high standard of neatness to the bereft Lincoln children. A school was opened in the community, and all five children attended. Abe grew taller and taller and attained great strength. He hired out for work and was popular with neighboring young people because of his humor and fair-mindedness. Intellectually curious, he read avidly and loved to talk. He seized an opportunity to make a trip to New Orleans on a flatboat of produce to sell. His stepmother testified later that "Abe was the best boy I ever saw or ever expect to see." [1]

Abe's sister Sarah married in 1826, but died in childbirth. Mrs. Lincoln's two daughters married and moved to Illinois. Enthusiastic reports of the fertility of the soil in Illinois, combined with Mrs. Lincoln's desire to live near her daughters, persuaded the Lincoln family in 1830 to move on. They crossed the Wabash at Vincennes. Abe was twenty-one and ready to go out on his own.

How did the Lincolns and their neighbors impress others? Morris Birkbeck, English Quaker, crossed the state in 1817 and observed,

> If I mistake not, the character of the settlers is different, and
> superior to that of the first settlers in Ohio, who were generally very
> indigent people: those who are now fixing themselves in Indiana
> bring with them habits of comfort and the means of producing the
> conveniences of life; I observe this in the construction of their

---

1. Louis A. Warren, *Lincoln's Youth: Indiana Years, Seven to Twenty-one, 1816–1830* (New York: Appleton, Century, Crofts, 1959), p. 212.

cabins and the neatness surrounding them, and especially in their well-stocked gardens, so frequent here and so rare in the state of Ohio.[2]

Dr. Richard Lee Mason of Maryland passed through the state in 1819 and acquired a contrary impression. "The people of Indiana differ widely from Kentuckians in habits, manners and even dialect. Whilst hospitality, politeness and good sense characterize Kentuckians, ignorance, impudence and laziness has stamped the Indianans." [3]

Another Englishman, Captain William Blane, visited Indiana in 1822. He was more perceptive. After traveling in Europe, he was not quite prepared for frontier conditions, such as impassable roads and crude accommodations. "The Western Americans, and particularly those of Indiana," he wrote, "are more rough and unpolished in their manners than those of any country I ever travelled in." True enough, no doubt, but then he made an interesting distinction:

> When I began to enter into the company of the Backwoodsmen, quite off the roads and where a traveller was seldom or never seen, I found the character of the settlers quite different from what I had supposed. In general they were open hearted and hospitable, giving freely whatever they had, and often refusing any recompense. It is true they always treated me as their equal; but at the same time, there was a sort of real civility in their behaviour, which I have often looked for in vain elsewhere . . . a degree of openness and hospitality, which indeed the most fastidious could not but have admired.[4]

Which observer deserves credence? We can't be sure; all we know for certain are a few basic figures that provide measurements but not values. The census of 1820 showed 147,500 people in the state, including more than 1,200 free Negroes and 190

2. Morris Birkbeck, *Notes on a Journey in America, from the Coast of Virginia to the Territory of Illinois* (Philadelphia: Caleb Richardson, 1817), p. 102.

3. Quoted in *Indiana as Seen by Early Travelers,* edited by Harlow Lindley (Indianapolis: Indiana Historical Commission, 1916), pp. 235–236.

4. William N. Blane, *An Excursion Through the United States and Canada, During the Years 1822–23* (London: Printed for Baldwin, Cradock, and Joy, 1824), pp. 140, 146.

contract slaves. The frontier period of imminent dangers was drawing to a close. Not only was Indiana a full-fledged state, but all along its western boundary loomed Illinois, which had entered the Union in 1818. There were Indians, still, in the northern part of Indiana, but they were no longer a menace. The great central third of the state, though wooded, was fertile and safe. That vast center region of Indiana, below the east-to-west flow of the Wabash River, was a New Purchase negotiated with the Miami, Kickapoo, Wea, and Delaware in 1818. The latter three tribes obtained annuities from Congress and left the state.

Clearing Indian title to the area encouraged those citizens who wanted the state capital relocated near the geographical center. The change was typical of a burgeoning state. Such a location would also put the capital near the forward edge of the northward thrust of settlement and encourage further advance toward Michigan Territory. In January 1820 the legislature provided for ten commissioners to select a site and lay out a new capital town, far from Corydon. The members rode to the west branch of White River and turned up Fall Creek. They passed occasional squatters, and in the midst of a semiclearing, they determined to locate the new site on a square mile. The assembly approved their choice in 1821 and named it Indianapolis. In Vincennes, the *Indiana Centinel & Public Advertiser* exploded:

> One of the most ludicrous acts, however, of the sojourners at Corydon, was their naming of the new seat of state government. Such a name, dear reader, you would never find by searching from Dan to Beersheba; nor in all the libraries, museums, and patent-offices in the world. It is like nothing in heaven nor on earth, nor in the waters under the earth. It is not a name for a man, woman or child; for empire, city, mountain or morass; for bird, beast, fish, nor creeping thing; and nothing mortal or immortal could have thought of it, except the wise men of the East who were congregated at Corydon. It is composed of the following letters:
>
> I-N-D-I-A-N-A-P-O-L-I-S! [5]

Obviously, the editor was no scholar of Greek.

The same General Assembly appointed a commission of three

5. January 13, 1821.

to lay out a town and sell lots. Former Lieutenant Governor Christopher Harrison, a native of Maryland and a bachelor living in Salem, was the most conscientious, going to the new site and taking with him two surveyors, Alexander Ralston and Elias P. Fordham. Ralston had worked with Pierre L'Enfant in designing Washington, D.C. He now planned the mile square for central Indianapolis. In the center he put a circle of four acres, 333 feet in diameter, with a ronde 80 feet wide. One street penetrated to the circle north and south on the meridian line and was named Meridian Street. Another reached the circle east and west and was called Market Street. One block south was the main thoroughfare, Washington Street, running east and west—and when most streets were hardly 30 feet across, it was 125 feet wide! The rest of the mile square was overlaid with a gridiron of nine streets running north and south and named originally for states. Another nine streets ran east and west. At each corner of the inner square, a diagonal street pushed out through the gridiron. As these streets were marked out, cabins of squatters had to be moved and trees felled.

An auction of lots was held in October 1821, when 314 tracts were sold. A double block was reserved for the capitol, and another block for a county courthouse, which would go up first. The circle was reserved for the governor's mansion, and here is where government planning went awry. A big, square, brick house was constructed. A door on each of the four sides opened into a long hallway, and the two halls crossed, cutting the house into four big rooms, upstairs as well as down. Like the modern Pittsburgh post office, in which slots for mailing letters were forgotten, the governor's mansion suffered from two curious omissions: there was no kitchen; and the house stood so publicly exposed that there was no backyard in which to hang the laundry. As a result, no governor would ever live there. Schoolboys broke into it, tramps slept in the basement, two or three bachelors rented rooms, and Judge Isaac Blackford spent some time there. It was torn down in 1857. Meanwhile, a new governor's house was bought in 1839 at the corner of Washington and Illinois.

The capitol, built between 1832 and 1835, was designed after

the Greek style by Towne and Davis of New York. It was an
imitation of the Parthenon, measuring one hundred feet wide by
two hundred feet long. It stood two stories high, and a high,
windowed dome had been added. The foundation was limestone, but the walls were lath, covered with stucco, which did
not wear well through the winter seasons. Fifty tall, fluted
columns marched in great dignity around the four sides. If
the design was not pure Greek, it was nevertheless a well-
proportioned and imposing building, handsomer by far than
the immense "General Grant-style" capitol that replaced it,
started in the late 1870s. Bulging and bulky on the outside, the
cavernous interior is so overwhelming as to be almost majestic.

Anticipating the importance of the new town, settlers flocked
in to establish stores and professions and to live in the capital. A
newspaper was started early in 1822, and a big Fourth-of-July
celebration was held. The town turned out for a community pic-
nic and ate a barbecued deer, killed just off Washington Street.
Fourteen toasts were drunk, one for each of the original thirteen
states and one for Indianapolis. In August the city voted in its
first election: 315 ballots for William Hendricks as governor,
and two against him. Statewide, he won. A revival, or pro-
tracted religious meeting, was held in September. One result
was establishment of churches by, first, a Baptist congregation,
and soon after by Presbyterians. A private school was opened.

The state records and treasury were moved from Corydon to
Indianapolis in wagons in October 1824, under the direction of
Samuel Merrill, the state treasurer. Merrill's family rode along,
and his little niece, Mary Catherine Anderson, remembered it
vividly:

> The road was laid with rails or logs for miles, then covered with
> water that seemed bottomless. When the horses and wagons would
> go down, it seemed they might have reached China. At such times,
> my sister would scream with fright. One day we traveled two miles
> and a half only. . . . I walked all the way, only when we came
> near Columbus, as it was raining. . . . Mr. Siebert (a driver) had a
> fashion of putting bells on his horses whenever we came near a

town. . . . So we went into the seat of the government with fine, large strong horses strung with bells, all ringing.[6]

The ten-day trek cost the state $118.07, minus proceeds from the sale of furniture at Corydon of $52.52, for a net cost of $65.55.

By 1827 the town had a population of a thousand, with twenty-five brick, sixty frame, and eighty hewn-log houses. That was also the year the National Road from Wheeling across Ohio was surveyed to Indianapolis—now no longer an isolated settlement in the wilderness. Twenty years passed before a railroad from Madison reached the capital and linked it to Ohio River traffic. By 1855, seven rail lines spread out like spokes from Indianapolis. It was clearly a transportation center, attractive to manufacturers as well as to farmers and retailers. It was ready for its slogan: "Crossroads of America."

To this new town came Calvin Fletcher, from Vermont—via Ohio, where he had sojourned to teach school, study law, and marry. Fletcher was representative of the New England and northern men who moved into Indiana and often achieved positions of influence beyond their proportion in the population. He arrived in Indianapolis in the fall of 1812 and settled into a log cabin. He engaged in the practice of law, served the circuit court for some twenty years, and was elected to the state senate in 1826. As he prospered, he bought a farm five miles outside town, though he continued to live in town with his growing family. Fletcher was early active in the Indiana Colonization Society and was elected a director of the State Bank. As a part-time farmer, he sought to improve farm production for everyone by promoting a county fair and helping to organize a county agricultural society. A Methodist, he participated in the opening of Asbury (DePauw) College. By 1846, he had fathered eleven children and sent several of his sons east to college.

Gradually, Fletcher withdrew from law practice and confined his work to farming and banking. People recognized his integ-

6. Gayle Thornbrough and Dorothy L. Riker, editors, *Readings in Indiana History* (Indianapolis: Indiana Historical Bureau, 1960), pp. 173–174.

rity and trusted his judgment. His New England standards in
business, education, and benevolence were respected. He opposed slavery and supported the temperance movement, aiding
several local charities, as well. He promoted free schools in Indianapolis and served as a school trustee. After the death of his
wife, in 1854, he married again. He joined the new Republican
party, warmly favored Lincoln, and was sent by Governor Morton to Canada in April 1861 to purchase arms for Indiana
troops. When Fletcher died, in 1866, the city lost a substantial
and progressive leader.

White dominance of Indiana proceeded relentlessly. After
1820, probably not more than three thousand Miami and Potawatomi Indians were left in the state. Their condition did not
make a pretty picture. The Reverend Isaac McCoy, Baptist missionary in the north, was depressed by widespread drunkenness
among the Indians and the crimes and cruelties that were committed during intoxication. If liquor was their downfall, McCoy
hoped that their removal to reservations, from which the traders
were excluded, might save them. Hugh McCulloch, who lived
in Fort Wayne, had a low opinion of those whites:

> As for the licensed traders, it can be safely said that they have been
> the reverse of what they ought to have been. Nor has dishonesty in
> trade with the Indians been confined to licensed traders. . . .
> Nothing surprised me more, as I became acquainted in the manner
> in which this trade was carried on, than the fact that men who had
> the reputation of dealing fairly with white men did not hesitate to
> practice the most shameful impositions in their dealings with the
> Indians.[7]

It is clear beyond a doubt that the Hoosiers did not think
much of the Indians and little more of the French, primarily
because, in terms of the American work ethic, both seemed
lazy. To the American pioneers, laziness was almost a sin,
because it meant not living up to one's capacity, not utilizing

7. Hugh McCulloch, *Men and Manners of Half a Century* (New York: C. Scribner's
Sons, 1888), p. 102.

God-given abilities, not garnering the fruits of God's bounty. Consequently, the pioneers thought that charity to such people was pointless and inappropriate. On the other hand, if there was anything to the idea of teaching by example, the Hoosiers would show their neighbors what a good life on the frontier could be with proper exertion.

Most of the French and most of the Indians did not elect to imitate the Anglo-American farmers and so were left economically further and further behind. There was no thought of dispossessing the few French in the area, who were turning to subsistence farming; their low economic status was viewed as the inevitable result of ignorance and indolence. Toward the Indians, the Anglo-American attitude was a great deal less tolerant. Yet, among themselves, where mutual respect prevailed, the Hoosiers could be admired.

Returning to the Indiana scene in 1827, the Reverend Isaac Reed expanded on Hoosier character.

> I had omitted to say anything of the hospitality which abounds, and may be considered as characteristical in Indiana. I have seen it in almost all parts of the State, in near a hundred different settlements; and I therefore believe it is general. . . . There is much equality among the people, especially in country neighborhoods. There is less absolute and suffering poverty than I have ever seen in so large a country; and a man is an idle and lazy fellow if he does not soon get a farm of his own. There are very few who are rich; and it is not easy to get rich there.[8]

Commenting on towns at that time, Timothy Flint, a Harvard graduate who, as a missionary, had traveled extensively in the Ohio and Mississippi valleys, had to admit of Indiana that

> None of the western states have shown a greater propensity for town making than this. Nature had furnished it with so many delightful sites for towns, that their frequency subtracts from the importance of any individual position. In no part of the world has the art of trumpeting and lauding the advantages, conveniences and future prospects of the town to be sold, been carried to greater perfection.

8. Quoted in Lindley, *Indiana as Seen by Early Travelers*, p. 504.

To mention in detail all the villages that have really attained some degree of consequence would only furnish a barren catalogue of names.[9]

Most of the new towns did follow repetitive patterns of founding and growth, but four spots around the state offered experiments in alternative living. One of them, established in 1825, was New Harmony, the dreamlike reverie of Robert Owen, a Welsh textile manufacturer motivated by an admirable desire to improve the life of factory workers. Two others—Mongo, established in 1841 in La Grange County, and the Philadelphia Industrial Association, founded near South Bend in 1845—were based on the social theories of Charles Fourier (1772–1837), an obscure French business broker turned social philosopher. A third, Moore's Hill Phalanx, begun in Dearborn County in 1857 by Alexander Longley, was based on the "Fourier Phalanx" idea.

Of the four, New Harmony, some fifty miles below Vincennes and thirty miles from Evansville, succeeded temporarily, due to the author's financial support, but internal dissension caused it to disband after only three years. The town itself, and its name, had been established originally about 1814 or 1815 by a religious group, German Separatists, led by a man named George Rapp. The group had first settled in Pennsylvania, founding a village they called Harmonie, or Harmony. Their religious beliefs were somewhat austere, and they held property in common. They prospered in Indiana, but nonetheless sold their holdings at New Harmony to Owen in 1825 and went back to Pennsylvania.

Owen paid them $95,000 for the land and buildings and $40,000 more for their livestock, implements, and a year's provisions for a thousand people. He believed that the key to Utopia was co-operation instead of competition, with necessities distributed according to need, education and entertainment provided, and the good life made available for contented and eager

9. Timothy Flint, *Recollections of the Last Ten Years* (Boston: Cummings, Hilliard and Co., 1826), p. 5.

workers. Before he had come to America, Owen had tried out his ideas in his place of business in Scotland: he had reduced the long hours of work, raised wages, eliminated child labor, built schools, and arranged better housing—and made it all pay. Nevertheless, his conservative partners had forced him out. Determined to start afresh with a new community in the New World, he bought the New Harmony property.

After advertising his plans (and winning a good press in the United States), Owen attracted a strange mixture of about a thousand persons to New Harmony. A few were educated scientists and teachers, others were earnest reformers of few practical skills, and still others were the dissatisfied, looking for an easy life. Owen had not counted on the possibility of laziness, incompetence, greed, or dishonesty appearing. Intellectually, much was achieved, largely through the efforts of William Maclure, a wealthy Scot interested in education. New Harmony boasted advanced schooling, scientific research, concerts and plays, a newspaper of superior content, a fine library, free discussion of reforms, festive parties, and stimulating conversations—cultural delights not found in any other community in Indiana or in the Old Northwest, outside of Cincinnati.

Economically, New Harmony was host to an extraordinary collection of misfits. Agricultural production by unskilled farmers failed to provide enough food to go around, let alone sell abroad. The industrious and responsible grew tired of supporting the lazy and contentious. They looked to Owen for further benefactions while they argued about the rules for their new society. Owen wanted to move teenagers of both sexes into central houses, supervised by one matron; and he proposed new styles of unisex dress that included pantaloons tied at the ankles for both women and men.

The evils of human nature seemed as prevalent in New Harmony as in competitive societies. Utopia always appeared just over the horizon. When Owen refused to hand out more money and returned to Great Britain in 1827, the noble experiment was finished. Everyone was disillusioned except Owen himself; he never admitted defeat. His four sons and his daughter remained to salvage his investment by selling properties to self-supporting families who wanted to stay.

The Owen children all distinguished themselves. Robert Dale Owen served three terms in the state legislature and two terms in Congress before participating in the Constitutional Convention of 1850–1851. He introduced the bill in 1845 that created the Smithsonian Institution, and he was a long-time champion of the property rights of married women and easier divorce laws for them. He was appointed minister to Naples in the 1850s, and during the Civil War he influenced Lincoln on emancipation and later investigated the condition of the freedmen.

David Dale Owen was state geologist in 1837 and became United States geologist ten years later. He also built a chemical laboratory for himself in New Harmony.

Richard Owen became a geologist in his brother David's employ, and during the Civil War was the humane commandant of Camp Morton (Indianapolis), whose rebel prisoners later contributed to a statue honoring him. For a decade he was professor of natural philosophy (physics) at Indiana University.

William Owen, who died in 1842, conducted the family's general store, helped organize the county agricultural society and the local thespian society, and served as a director of the State Bank of Indiana.

Jane Dale Owen married Robert Fauntleroy, gave music lessons, and conducted a girls' boarding school in New Harmony. Largely through their leadership, the town retained its cultural bent, if not its level.

Charles Fourier's utopian communities at Mongo and South Bend were founded some years later. Fourier had tried to establish one association in 1832, but failed in that attempt. Having lived through the French Revolution and the Napoleonic wars, he was pessimistic about the future unless men would "condemn the whole system of society itself." [10] He wanted to substitute co-operation and united industry for individualism and

10. Arthur E. Bestor, Jr., *Backwoods Utopias* (Philadelphia: University of Pennsylvania Press, 1950), p. 8.

competition, and incidentally he would "free the passions."
Getting down to practical plans, he would gather people into
"phalanxes" or economic units of 1,600 each, and each phalanx would inhabit a common building. Most members should
be devoted to agriculture, but some might pursue other occupations. In fact, members might move from one job to another at
will. Family life could continue, but marriage was abolished as
a restraint. From the harvest, a subsistence was furnished each
person, and the surplus was distributed according to labor, talent, and capital. Fourier was a bit vague about that.

What was most remarkable about Fourier was his ignorance
of the way society had evolved and his blindness to the re-
straints in his own system. Yet he made one disciple of a well-
educated young American studying in Europe—Albert Brisbane, whose fervor was not matched by either sophistication or
leadership. Rather, Brisbane preferred to propagandize "practical associations" as a panacea for all the evils of society made
apparent by rising industrialism. His book *The Social Destiny of
Man* appeared in 1840. "The root of the evil is in the social organization itself," he declared, not "in the imperfection of
human nature." [11] Brisbane was supported by Horace Greeley,
New York editor, who should have known better, and to his
surprise, he inspired about forty phalanxes in this country, including Brook Farm, a group of intellectuals in Massachusetts.
These experiments all failed, eventually, including three in Indiana.

The first Fourier phalanx in Indiana was the one established at
Mongo, and it attracted somewhat more than a hundred joiners.
The second was the Philadelphia Industrial Association, located
on the edge of South Bend. The third was Moore's Hill Phalanx, begun by Alexander Longley, who started nearly a dozen
utopian colonies with his wife's money and never learned anything from their failures.

In the case of New Harmony and the phalanxes, the rock of

11. Albert Brisbane, *The Social Destiny of Man: Or, Association and Reorganization
of Industry* (Philadelphia: C. F. Stollmeyer, 1840), p. 27.

individualism that they were designed to shatter proved harder than any social theorist had imagined. Owen and Fourier and Brisbane could explicate endlessly on social goals and organization, yet none of them recognized individual aspirations or weaknesses, because they would not believe that society was shaped by them. Getting the cart before the horse, they insisted that social organization completely shaped individuals. Anyway, hundreds of Hoosiers tried the co-operative life briefly and decided that it was not for them.

The social experiments Indiana has harbored suggest both a restlessness and an open-mindedness toward new ideas and even eccentricity. Their failure indicates that they were part of Indiana's growing up. By the time of the Civil War, Hoosiers were committed to the orthodox American system of independent family life and responsibility and of private enterprise with its competition and individual striving.

The traditional style of family living retained its attraction and was continually reinforced by surging newcomers. The census of 1830 showed that the population—343,000—had more than doubled in a decade. No other state received such a percentage increase. While the southern counties grew by 50 percent, the central counties jumped by 600 percent. The population had become predominantly, almost exclusively, white, and even the fringe of Indians was doomed.

The state assembly had petitioned Congress in 1829 for removal of the last resident Indians, stating baldly that "so large a space of the best soil," impeded the development of internal improvements and the Indians needed protection from indolent and vicious habits to which, by their vicinity to our population, they are unhappily inclined." [12] Morally, it was felt that both races would benefit. Governor James B. Ray was a particular advocate of removal. It was enough in his eyes that "these creatures" impeded "the prosperity of our citizens." He argued that "a trial for half a century, to better their condition as independent nations, or tribes, has only served to increase their future

12. Indiana, *Laws of Indiana, 1828–1829*, p. 155.

wretchedness. They have, by some unaccountable fatality, acquired all of the vices of the whites, with but few of their virtues." [13] The gulf between the two cultures could not be bridged.

Black Hawk's war in 1832 gave impetus to the demands, although Indiana's Indians did not participate. President Andrew Jackson, the great champion of the common man, was never a champion of the Indians. He wanted to get rid of them. Several treaties were made in the next few years with various bands in Indiana who sought more and more money before agreeing to abandon the land of their ancestors. Small migrations took place over a decade, although most of the Potawatomi left before 1838. The largest group, from around Plymouth, under Chief Menominee, were forcibly removed. It was not a pleasant exodus; the Indians were marched out under militia guard. The trek of 860 to Kansas was called "The Trail of Death," as 30 perished during the two months on the way. The Indians were accompanied by their Catholic missionary, Father Benjamin Petit. A few of the Potawatomi escaped and returned to Indiana, where they settled again. Another 525 departed without incident from northern Indiana between South Bend and Fort Wayne in 1840.

The Miami left in 1846, escorted on board canal boats to Toledo, then to the Ohio and Mississippi, and finally up the Missouri to Kansas. A few were exempted and given land around Huntington and Fort Wayne. One result was that there were Indian children in the public schools in the first part of the twentieth century, and when the Indian Claims Commission allowed compensatory damages to the Miami in 1969 and 1972, mixed-bloods in Indiana shared in those awards.

Throughout most of the first half of the nineteenth century, there crossed and recrossed Indiana a strange figure of a man, scattering good and leaving a delicious heritage. His name was

13. Indiana, General Assembly, House of Representatives, *Indiana House Journal, 1829–30*, p. 36.

John Chapman, and he had come from Massachusetts to Pennsylvania and thence down the Ohio River to Ohio and the Indiana Territory. His constant love was fruit trees, his religion was Swedenborgian, and his costume was his own. The combination made him the eccentric, gentle, widely loved "Johnny Appleseed," and he became an enduring folk hero. By vocation, he was a nurseryman who planted his seeds on other men's lands, gave them half the trees, and sold the others as he could. But he gave away as much as he sold, and he planted appleseeds in advanced areas not yet settled, so that fruit would be available when the settlers came. "Comfort me with apples," he quoted from the Old Testament. Johnny went barefoot much of the year, wore a cooking pot on his head for his cornmeal mush, and always carried a bag of apple seeds. He took his meals at friendly cabins and kept on the move. He was never armed; Indians protected him, pioneers loved him, and children were enchanted by his stories. He died in 1845, about seventy years of age, near Fort Wayne, and he was buried there. Thousands of apple trees remained his true memorial. His saintly life became legendary and inspired a poem by Vachel Lindsay.

By 1840, perhaps four-fifths of the public land in Indiana had been sold to settlers or donated to state or local agencies. The census of that year again showed a doubling of the population, which reached 686,000. The southern and central regions were about equal in size, while the northern part, after the Indians' departure, showed 66,000. Indiana was to a substantial degree a southern state, inasmuch as those settlers born in the South or those who had lived there for a time after being born elsewhere probably constituted more than half of the 1840 population.[14] Farming predominated in the state, of course, and there were no real cities.

The effort to move crops to higher-priced markets and obtain manufactured goods at lower prices prompted every governor to

14. This calculation was worked out by John D. Barnhart and Donald F. Carmony in their *Indiana from Frontier to Industrial Commonwealth,* 4 vols. (New York: Lewis Historical Publishing Company, 1954), 1: 178.

urge internal improvements, by which they meant improved transportation. Roads were first built from the 5 percent revenue received from sale of lands granted to the state by Congress, plus a local road tax, plus a requirement that men between the ages of eighteen and fifty must work for the state six days a year. Then the federal government started the National Road from Wheeling across Ohio; it reached Indiana in 1827 and was continued westward. The Michigan Road, from Madison to Indianapolis to Michigan City, was begun in 1838 at state expense.

The Wabash and Erie Canal was a joint undertaking of Indiana, Ohio, and the federal government. It was started at Fort Wayne in 1832 and proceeded in both directions at once, but it took ten years to reach Toledo on the east and Lafayette on the west. The Indiana General Assembly chartered eight railroad companies, five of which were to connect Indianapolis with ports on the Ohio River. The general outlook was as enthusiastic as it was visionary. In 1836 the assembly passed a bill calling for eight internal improvements simultaneously: extension of the Wabash and Erie Canal to Terre Haute, a Central Canal from the Wabash River through Indianapolis to Evansville, a Whitewater Canal from Cambridge City through Brookville to Lawrenceburg, a railroad from Madison through Indianapolis to Lafayette, a macadamized road from New Albany to Vincennes via Paoli and Washington, the removal of obstructions to navigation in the Wabash River, a survey for a railroad or canal from Jeffersonville to Crawfordsville, and an eventual survey for a canal or railroad from Fort Wayne to Michigan City. Almost every region got something in the bill; that was its fatal defect.

The appropriation for the eight projects amounted to $10 million, to be derived from the sale of state bonds bearing 5 percent interest and payable in twenty-five years. That would require $500,000 a year (5 percent of $10 million) to be paid out to bond holders. The total annual state income was only about $75,000; the rest had to come from profits of these transport lines. However, construction costs exceeded estimates, and maintenance (the destructiveness of muskrats had not been considered) ate up all the profits. Overextended, Indiana defaulted on its bonds in 1840 and was virtually bankrupt. It turned over the improvement projects to any private company that would complete them. The great casualty of this delirium was Indiana's credit. The Wabash and Erie Canal was extended to Terre Haute by 1849 and to Evansville by 1853. It was dug largely by Irishmen, who fought as lustily as they dug. Of great benefit to farmers, the canal was used even after sections of it were closed after 1874. The Whitewater Canal was finally completed, but went bankrupt in 1862. The only successful project was the railroad out of Madison that reached Indianapolis in 1847; by 1855, six other rail lines built privately spread out of the city.

The financial debacle of internal improvements frightened Hoosiers about the power of government to make wrong business decisions and to defraud bond holders. The state had exhausted its financial resources by spending money on the wrong improvements first: it should have built schools and railroads. The political effect was to prohibit the state under its second constitution from going in debt.

Some diversion was provided by the Mexican War. In May 1846, Secretary of War William L. Marcy called for three regiments from Indiana. The state's militia system had been largely abandoned, and there were no arms and no money. Four banks lent Governor James Whitcomb $35,000 for equipment and transportation. Young Lew Wallace began recruiting. The First Regiment was ready by the middle of June and started south. They were stationed on the Rio Grande for the duration, to the great disgust of Lieutenant Wallace. The Second and Third regiments were organized later and saw action. Although the Third performed very well, the Second Regiment made a poor showing at Buena Vista in February 1847, by reason of the incompetence of its colonel, who was found wanting in capacity and judgment by a court of inquiry. More than five hundred men died of disease or were killed; it was not a war to arouse any militarism or pride in Indiana, and the Gold Rush and the rising slavery controversy made it easy to forget.

The census of 1850 was the first to show the origins of the country's inhabitants. The total did not double again, for Indiana; the increase dropped to 50 percent. Among Indiana's one million population, more than half—541,000—were born in the state, a second and third generation of natives. Another 400,000 were born in other states. These two groups totalled 92 percent of the inhabitants; 11,200 were free Negroes, or about 1 percent. The remainder were foreign-born, made up principally of 28,500 Germans, stolid farmers and craftsmen; 12,800 Irish, chiefly diggers of canals and layers of railroad tracks; and 7,000 British and Canadians. Indiana stood seventh in population among the states. Over 95 percent of these people resided in what were called rural areas.

The "cities" of Indiana were urban centers only by loose application of the word. The three biggest towns were New Albany, Indianapolis, and Madison, with approximately equal populations ranging from 8,000 to 8,180 each. Next came Lafayette, with 6,100; then Terre Haute and Fort Wayne, with 4,000 each, and Evansville with 3,600. These towns were markets and trade centers, dependent on the surrounding farms and cherishing rural traditions. It was the Golden Age of agriculture; Indiana stood third among states in production of hogs, fourth in corn, fifth in sheep, and sixth in wheat.

But the Golden Age had its cancer—the slavery issue—and Indiana could not isolate itself from the darkening controversy. Increasing enforcement of the Fugitive Slave Law antagonized Hoosiers. In Indianapolis in 1853 a case of mistaken identity of a free Negro who was claimed by a Kentuckian was the talk of the state. The Negro was released, and the Kentuckian had to sneak out of the city at night. Still, Indiana was something of a game preserve for honest and dishonest Southerners hunting their slaves. The explanation lay partly in the state's location on a direct route for slaves fleeing from the South to Michigan, Canada, and freedom, and partly in the activities in Indiana of Levi Coffin.

Coffin came to Fountain City (old Newport) in 1826, where he found that escaping slaves were being aided by free Negroes. He and his wife were Quakers from North Carolina, where they had been helping slaves start their escape route northward for a dozen years. Now at the other end of the line, Coffin organized what was dubbed an "underground railroad," to run from the Ohio River to Michigan. There were "depots" every fifteen or twenty miles, where families would shelter slaves over the daylight hours and guide them to the next depot at night. More than 250 Hoosiers were involved in the operation, but the majority of people knew nothing about it. The women made clothes for the fugitives. It has been estimated that at least 2,000 slaves were put up at Coffin's house alone.

The Quakers of the area, by and large, objected to abolitionism, and Coffin was "read out of meeting" for his radical and illegal actions. The so-called president of the underground railroad eventually moved to Cincinnati in 1847 to undertake a larger antislavery work. At length he was reinstated in his church.

A weak antislavery society favoring "colonization" had been organized in 1838 among the Quakers in Indiana, and the state was viewed with some misgiving by other northern states. Most Hoosiers favored sending the slaves back to Africa rather than granting immediate freedom here. The colonization group was most active in the early 1840s, helping to split church denominations between North and South, then turning to political action through the Liberty party. That party in Indiana held its state convention in Fountain City in 1842 and nominated a candidate for governor.

After the Mexican War, citizens became absorbed in obtaining a constitutional convention and writing a new state charter, which was completed in 1851. But then came the Kansas-Nebraska Bill of 1853, in Congress. Under the Missouri Compromise of 1820, a precarious peace had been maintained by an agreement that, west of Missouri, new land north of 36 degrees, 30 minutes would be free of slavery, while states emerging to the south of that could have slaves. But when an interest in attempting a transcontinental railroad required some sort of organization of the central plains, proslavery Congressmen objected to the creation of a territorial government in what would become a free state. To placate the Southerners, a Congressional committee under U.S. Senator Stephen A. Douglas of Illinois suggested that the area be broken into two territories—Kansas and Nebraska—in which the settlers would determine whether slavery should be permitted or excluded. That was the doctrine of popular sovereignty, and it nullified the old Compromise. After bitter debate, the bill passed in 1854. It was conceded that Nebraska would be a free territory, but opposing factions rushed to settle Kansas (which lay north of 36 degrees, 30 minutes) in order to influence the popular decision about slavery. They fought each other, each faction drawing up a constitution.

That controversy was followed in 1856 by Dred Scott's appeal to the U.S. Supreme Court concerning his status. A slave, Scott had been taken to Minnesota for several years, then back to a slave state. He sued for his freedom because he had once lived in an area where slavery was illegal. The court ruled in March 1857 that Scott was still a slave. The decision had the effect of again nullifying the Missouri Compromise and fanned the flames of sectional antagonism.

The Old Whigs and Liberty party men of Indiana vigorously opposed the Kansas-Nebraska Act, and so did some Democrats. But Indiana's two Democratic senators and all but two of its Democratic congressmen voted for the bill. Their stand brought about the defeat of the Democratic party in the state election of 1854, and only one of the Democratic representatives in Congress survived. Yet Indiana did not commit herself irrevocably to the antislavery position. In 1856 the Democrats regained control of the state, and the new Republican party managed to keep only one U.S. senator and five congressmen.

The Dred Scot decision, coming after the election, was highly unpalatable in Indiana. The Democratic party had little choice but to endorse it, along with popular sovereignty in the territories, even though Democratic newspapers in the state found it reprehensible. The Republicans condemned both the court and the new doctrine of local sovereignty. The state was definitely divided as the decade ran out.

In common with most other white Americans of that time,

Hoosiers were not racially tolerant: they didn't like Indians, and they didn't like Negroes. They had largely ousted Indians from the area, and had, by stipulations in the new constitution, forbidden Negroes to enter the state. The Hoosier attitude was based on limited personal contact and memories of past encounters with both races. Yet most Indiana whites did not want to see minority races abused or deprived of their rights. They remained suspicious of Roman Catholics, whose numbers doubled as more German and Irish immigrants poured in, but the foreign-born remained a small segment, 9 percent of the 1860 population, half of them in the southern part of the state.

The steady push northward of Southerners, and their spilling over into Illinois, had not gone unnoticed in New England. Puritan Yankees remembered that they had once been inspired not only to set a city on a hill, but to lead a new nation in godliness. The opening of the Northwest challenged them afresh. At first, it was a group of New England war veterans who founded Marietta and flocked to Cincinnati. The state of Connecticut held on to a Western Reserve along the south shore of Lake Erie for its citizens. Yankees and Yorkers foresaw that the West would eventually affect the entire country and that the area would be "just what the *people* of the West make it; and *they* will be what the influences sent out from the East make them." [15] Not from the South, but the East. What Dr. R. L. Power called the Yankee instinct for meddling rose from self-righteousness. Since the Southerners coming northward were, in Yankee eyes, poor, ignorant, shiftless, intemperate, profane, unconcerned about education or true religion, Indiana and Illinois must be "saved" from becoming outposts of Southern culture.

The Yankees sent missionaries and schoolteachers, urged group migrations, and promoted schools and colleges. Those who came to settle usually brought more goods—furniture, implements, tools, utensils—and more money than the Southern

15. Richard Lyle Power, *Planting Corn Belt Culture* (Indianapolis: Indiana Historical Society, 1953), p. 5.

immigrants. They took up better land. Where they settled in groups, they usually dominated the new community. Their literacy made them leaders. They found their Southern neighbors as odd as the Southerners found them, in outlook, speech, manners, foods, farm ways, and worship.

Never were the Yankees and their Yorker descendants very numerous, but when the Civil War came in 1861 and both Indiana and Illinois remained staunchly loyal to the Union, certain New Englanders, recalling three decades of mission in the West, rejoiced—incredibly—that they had won a modern "Thirty Years War." It was a conceit and a delusion. Not so much New England influence, but that of upland Southerners kept Indiana in the Union. Although settlers from the East and the South had intermingled and even intermarried, what is more significant is that the new state had shaped and colored both groups, stamping its own cultural identity on them. They would not shrink from war.

Despite all the differences and disagreements of the 1850s, a general air of optimism prevailed in Indiana because of Hoosier prosperity. There were roads to markets and land enough for all who were ambitious. Railroad-building had laid more than 2,100 miles of track in the state by 1860, and the lines running south and north were crossed by east-west lines in the upper half that now connected Hoosier farmers with eastern markets and diminished dependence on southern outlets. With 1,350,000 inhabitants, Indiana rose to sixth rank in the Union. In crops, it stood second among the states in wheat production, third in hogs, fourth in corn, and seventh in sheep. The environment generally was kind, and a comfortable living was within reach of the enterprising. This Golden Decade of agriculture had only another year to run before it was darkened by war.

The Kentucky boy who had grown up in Indiana was elected president in 1860. He carried the state with more votes than his three rivals combined, and he lifted a Republican governor into office.

Secession from the Union began before President Lincoln was

inaugurated. Voices in Indiana's southern counties, which were Democratic, anyway, argued that the state's true interest lay with the South. A few strong minds in the region, however, were ardent Unionists and agreed with Governor Oliver P. Morton that coercion against the seceders was simply enforcement of the law. "If it was worth a bloody struggle to establish this nation," he declared, "it is worth one to preserve it." [16]

A bloody struggle it was, and destined to redefine Indiana. The toll was enormous, and the intensity of the war effort hid the lasting significance of the conflict for some time. A glance at the consuming fire should precede consideration of its effects. Not foreseen was Governor Morton's capacity for leadership in a crisis. When war came and he was informed that Indiana's quota of soldiers was 4,683, he promptly offered 12,000 state troops. Of indubitable courage, he threw himself into the war struggle with extraordinary energy and marvelous organizing ability, untrammeled by the slightest self-doubt. While some people wrung their hands or stood on the sidelines, Morton plunged into the thick of things and soon was directing every turn. He moved everywhere, to camps, hospitals, battlefields, to the national Capitol and back again. He borrowed money personally to buy arms and start a state arsenal to make ammunition. He transformed the state fairgrounds into a training camp. He looked after the soldiers, saw to their welfare, their hospital care, and their dependents, until his name drew cheers from any Indiana regiment. Morton always knew what needed to be done, and he did it, or ordered others to do it. For four long years, Lincoln endured his recommendations, his complaints, his dire prophecies, all delivered by telegram when not by personal visit. The state's Democrats saw what he was achieving in political devotion and could only gnash their teeth. If they uttered complaints, Morton was quick to call them obstructionists and even traitors. He could sell himself to the soldiers and their fam-

16. William Dudley Foulke, *Life of Oliver P. Morton*, 2 vols. (Indianapolis-Kansas City: The Bowen-Merrill Co., 1899), 1: 93.

ilies, but he could not impress many of his political colleagues at home or his superiors in Washington.

Other Indianans besides the gubernatorial gadfly made major but less well-publicized contributions to the war effort. The Studebaker brothers at South Bend, for instance, earned national recognition for the army wagons they built, and the Van Camp Company in Indianapolis developed a new ration for the troops—canned pork and beans.

Statistics are heartless and inhuman, yet they summarize in brief and measurable terms Indiana's tremendous war service. The state furnished more soldiers and sailors to the Union forces in proportion to its population than any other northern state save one.[17] Much of that commitment must be credited to the enthusiasm and urging of Governor Morton. Altogether, Indiana raised 129 infantry regiments, 13 cavalry regiments, 1 regiment of heavy artillery, and 26 batteries of light artillery. These units totalled 196,363 men, by one count; but W. H. H. Terrell, the governor's military secretary and afterward adjutant general of the state, showed the troop count at 208,367.[18] Almost 1,100 were sailors and marines, and more than 1,500 were Negroes.

Hoosier soldiers were active in all theaters of the war, fighting in more than three hundred engagements. They first saw action in western Virginia, fought Stonewall Jackson in the Shenandoah Valley, and then were active in the Peninsular campaign. Five regiments fought at Antietam in September 1862 and were bloodied again at Fredericksburg and Chan-

17. One way of figuring is to count all men who enlisted or were drafted and those who paid substitutes or commutation fines. These totals show that Delaware furnished 74.8 percent of its men of military age, and Indiana was immediately behind with 74.3 percent. See William F. Fox, *Regimental Losses in the American Civil War, 1861–65* (Albany: Albany Publishing Co., 1889), pp. 535–536. Another statistical procedure is to count only those white men who served three years or more, which shows Kansas furnishing 59.4 percent of its men of military age, and Indiana next, with 57 percent.

18. Terrell issued *Indiana in the War of the Rebellion* (Indianapolis: Douglass and Conner, Printers, 1869), later published as volume one of *The Report of the Adjutant General of the State of Indiana* (Indianapolis: A. H. Conner, State Printer, 1869).

cellorsville and at Gettysburg. These were the Seventh, Four-teenth, Nineteenth, Twentieth, and Twenty-seventh. The Nine-teenth was one of three regiments that constituted the famous Iron Brigade. It and the Twentieth and Twenty-seventh suffered the highest losses of all Indiana regiments during the war.

Most of Indiana's troops served west of the Appalachians. They fought in Missouri and Arkansas, served under Grant at Fort Donelson and Shiloh, where fourteen Indiana regiments took part in the battle and suffered a tenth of all casualties there. They lost heavily in half a dozen battles in Kentucky, were at the siege of Vicksburg, and suffered more than 3,000 casualties at Chickamauga. They climbed Lookout Mountain and followed Sherman to Atlanta. Forty-eight Indiana regiments stormed Kennesaw Mountain and lost severely. After Atlanta fell, half of the state's regiments pursued Hood back to Nashville and crushed him. The regiments in the East followed Grant through the Wilderness campaign and the ultimate capture of Richmond. About 5 percent, or 10,000, are listed as having deserted.

The Indiana regiments were, in general, well led; but few of those colonels advanced to become distinguished generals. Lew Wallace, Robert Milroy, and Joseph J. Reynolds became re-spected major generals. In the final months of the war, twenty Indiana officers were recognized by being brevetted major gen-erals; thirty-six attained the rank of brigadier general.

Indiana escaped being a battlefield except for a couple of epi-sodes. Kentucky was a divided state, and every time Confeder-ate forces invaded it, the Ohio River towns of Indiana grew apprehensive and feared invasion. Once, in July 1862, some thirty militia from Kentucky conducted a raid on Newburgh, east of Evansville. It was a one-day, plundering affair, and local militia, known as the Republican Wide-awakes, were ineffec-tual in defense. There was a comic-opera aspect to the brief event. Then early in July 1863, General John Hunt Morgan, an inspiring and overindependent Confederate cavalry leader in Kentucky and Tennessee, lacking in good judgment, could not resist the lure of a raid into Indiana. His purpose, or what he hoped to accomplish, has never been clarified, and he disobeyed the orders of his superior, General Braxton Bragg, not to cross the river. The movement followed upon the fall of Vicksburg to Grant and the costly Battle of Gettysburg to Lee.

Morgan took about 3,000 men across the Ohio from Brandenburg to Mauckport on July 8 and then set out northward. The first town he came to was Corydon. Barely forewarned, the local militia threw together a road barrier, while 400 of them barricaded themselves around the Old Capital. The Kentucky horsemen hardly hesitated and, with carbines firing, dispersed the defenders and rode into town, where the bastioned militia surrendered and were paroled.[19] The troopers disported themselves by raiding the stores, robbing the county treasury, and demanding ransom for grist mills that otherwise would be burned. They also carried off such impractical items as bolts of calico, streaming behind from one end tied to their saddles. One man carried a bird cage with three canaries in it for two days. The pattern was beginning to set.

Morgan had to live off the country; he needed food and fresh mounts as his horses gave out. Along the way, his cavalry burned a couple of houses, several bridges and water tanks, but offered no violence to women. Proceeding usually in two columns, they sent out detachments to comb the country five miles on either side of their route. Thus they stole horses over a ten-mile swath, making no distinction between Southern sympathizers and Unionists.

Governor Morton, who had had word of the invasion before Morgan reached Corydon, called out the militia. More than 60,000 men began to gather, half expecting Morgan to approach Indianapolis. None got to impede the Confederate's route because, with telegraph lines cut, they could not anticipate his

19. A friend of mine years ago in Corydon found an elderly man who had been a teen-aged militiaman at the road blockade. My friend tried to draw him out by asking, "What did you do when you saw Morgan's men riding toward you?" The old veteran did not hesitate: "I run like hell," he said, "just like ever'body else did!"

movement. From Kentucky, Brigadier Generals Edward Hobson and James Shackelford took up the pursuit, starting twenty-four hours after Morgan and needing as many remounts as he did.

Morgan's men went only as far north as Salem, turning east through New Philadelphia and Lexington, then north again to Dupont, which they reached early on Sunday morning, July 12. Discovering a packing house containing 2,000 hams, the troopers not only gathered them up, but the officers required the village wives to prepare a ham breakfast for them. The meat packer's daughter was as outraged and defiant as she was brave, and from a porch she told a group of Confederates what she thought of their ruinous thievery. One Kentucky trooper was enchanted by her spirited outburst. He spoke up in admiration: "After we git through lickin' you Yankees, I'm gonna come back up here and marry you!" He did, too, and their descendants still live in the vicinity.[20]

The hard-riding Union troops were only five hours behind Morgan at Dupont. Both forces were staying twenty-one hours a day in the saddle. Morgan swept northward to Vernon, seizing more money, then turned east to Versailles, where he robbed the county treasury. Being directly west of Cincinnati, he had to swing northeastward around the city. Accordingly, he crossed the Whitewater River at Harrison and burned the bridge. General Shackelford was only one hour behind him now, but the river crossing delayed the Union pursuers. Morgan left Indiana on Monday night, July 13, having accomplished little. In Ohio his command was divided; some escaped back to Kentucky, others were captured. Morgan himself was finally brought to bay on July 26 in northeastern Ohio. Imprisoned, he escaped in November and was given another command. He was killed in 1864 by Union troops who had penetrated Confederate lines at Greeneville, Tennessee.

The Civil War had greater impact on Indiana than any other war. The state paid a high toll in casualties for its generous par-

20. Edison H. Thomas, *John Hunt Morgan and His Raiders* (Lexington: University Press of Kentucky, 1975), p. 81.

ticipation. The 1860 population of 1,350,000 was diminished by the death of 24,400 young men—12 percent of those who fought. Never mind that half of them died ingloriously of disease in camp and hospital. The loss to farms and towns was devastating. In the War of 1812, probably fewer than 50 natives were killed. In the Mexican War, where disease took its toll, 510 lives were lost. In World War I, with a population twice that of the Civil War, Indiana lost 3,350 out of 118,000 men and women who served, or 2.8 percent. In World War II, from a population in 1941 of 3,500,000, the state lost about 10,000 out of roughly 340,000 men and women in service, or 3 percent. About 1,000 lives were lost in the Korean War. It is a wonder how the state recovered after 1865, but the Victorian sentimentalization of death helped make it bearable. The loss helps explain the fervor subsequently attending the Grand Army of the Republic, the pension legislation, the Memorial Day tributes, the soldiers' homes, and the veneration accorded the survivors at reunions.

The Civil War dispelled psychologically the notion that Indiana was an extension of the South, or even of the antislavery South, above the Ohio River. Several river towns and counties had fostered that view and felt that, because the state's culture was essentially Southern, its destiny was or should be linked with Kentucky. Both Governor Morton and the widespread military commitment to crushing the rebellion identified Indiana as an ardent Northern state, morally sympathetic to New England. Bitterness toward "Copperheads" (Northerners sympathetic with the South) in the southern part of the state kept antagonism toward Southerners alive for years. Indianapolis also rejected everything the Deep South stood for politically. Its economy was going to bind it to the Midwest.

The war glorified the Republican party and gave it a proud heritage, even though Hoosiers did not reward it with a steady majority. Twice before 1912, Indiana voted Democratic, then began to swing between the two parties, not always on the winning side. Both national parties, in seeking electoral votes, would frequently offer nominations to Hoosiers in order to carry

Indiana; they did so in 1868, 1876, 1880, 1888, 1892, 1904, 1908, 1912, and 1916.

Finally, the Civil War, along with the state's railroads, focused attention in Indiana on manufacturing and the benefits of future industrial development. In 1860, more than 91 percent of the population lived on farms or in towns of fewer than 2,500 residents. The 8.6 percent that was urban lived in small cities: Indianapolis was the largest, with 18,000 inhabitants; New Albany had 12,600; Evansville, 11,500; and Fort Wayne, 10,000. Farm-market towns would remain small, but cities that attracted factories would grow rapidly—a condition that was true of much of the country. The pattern of living in Indiana was going to change.

Part II

4

Hoosiers in Church and School

S historian Carl Becker pointed out decades ago, frontiersmen are men of faith. They do not see either the wilderness or themselves as they are, but as they will become. The frontier was the Promised Land, which could not be entered save by those who had faith. They were idealists, believing in the perfectibility of man and hence in both individualism and reform—but not in tolerance. Toleration implies a critical and speculative outlook, a suspension of judgment, or indifference; whereas frontiersmen have too intense a faith and too much idealism to be either hesitant or indifferent. New land to settle invites and encourages strong individuals of quick, sure judgments who tend to think alike. They have to possess courage, perseverance, industry, mutual concern, and they respect others who have the same qualities.

That analysis seems to fit Indiana. The early settlers had moral standards, but they were not equally devoted to church membership. Churches were scarce, of course; even back East, a very small percentage of the people were members. Roman Catholics predominated in Indiana in the eighteenth century, since the inhabitants were almost exclusively French, and the few Indians who professed Christianity were also Catholic. A Jesuit served Vincennes as early as 1749, and intermittently thereafter a priest was on duty. Baptists from Kentucky first formed a church in 1798 east of Charlestown. The oldest Protestant church building still on its original site is the Little Cedar Grove Baptist Church, three miles southeast of Brookville, erected in 1812. Methodist circuit riders came into southern Indiana and organized a church in 1801 at Springville, just west of Charlestown. Presbyterians were found among the Scotch-Irish from Pennsylvania, and a church was formed in 1806 near Vincennes. In the next year the Quakers who had entered the upper Whitewater valley set up their first meetinghouse at Richmond.

The Reverend Isaac Reed, a Presbyterian missionary from New York, wrote in 1819: "I have travelled considerably in new settlements in other parts, besides Indiana, but have never found so great numbers who seem to be religiously inclined, and who are professors of some sort, as in Indiana." [1] He himself formed eight churches in the state.

By 1820, Indiana's inhabitants were in large part extreme Arminians in theology, whether they knew it or not. Not for them was predestined election, a mysterious caprice of God, but everyone could achieve regeneration and salvation for himself by confession and good works. Their faith was consistent with their frontier experience, and the circuit riders of the Methodist denomination preached that good works would be rewarded. Nature was a challenge; men were judged on what they did with it. A corollary of that belief was the message of the Old Testament that the earth was provided for man to exploit. Further, like forests and swamps and wild animals, the Indians, too, were obstacles to be removed. They were also probably minions of the Devil, there to be regenerated by Christianity and agriculture if possible, or forced out, if not; tolerance of willful heathen was no virtue at all. The real virtues were good works, industry, perseverance, and faith in the future. Ultimately, these were regarded as American virtues. They left no room for predestination, servility to creeds or priests, and other-worldly concerns.

Religion was manifested in various ways, however, and some

1. Quoted in Lindley, *Indiana as Seen by Early Travelers*, p. 482.

extraordinary groups with remarkable theologies appeared in early Indiana. The Shakers established a community in 1808 on Busseron Creek, sixteen miles north of Vincennes, near its confluence with the Wabash River. It was called West Union, to distinguish it from Union Village near Lebanon, Ohio, founded in 1805. The official name of the group was the United Society of Believers in Christ's Second Appearing, a sect that diverged from a branch of the Society of Friends in England in the 1740s. Ann Lee, a convert of 1758, and a few followers brought the new faith to New York City in 1774, after she received a revelation directing her to go to America. The first community was established on a tract where Watervliet, near Albany, now stands. Ann Lee, using her maiden name after her husband left her in 1776 but better known as Mother Ann, joined her followers on the northern site. After the Revolution, she toured New England, making converts until her death in 1784. Her successors gathered the Believers into communal groups numbering eleven, augmented later by seven more communities in Ohio and Kentucky.

The Shakers believed in the duality of God as both eternal father and eternal mother. The English group expected Christ to reappear soon in female form, but Ann Lee had a vision that New Testament prophesy had already been fulfilled. In short, she was He. Yet neither Jesus nor Mother Ann was worshipped, but both were revered as elders. Singing hymns, confessing sins, speaking in tongues, and group dancing "to shake off the devil" were part of their religious ritual, and they became known as the Shaking Quakers—later, simply the Shakers. The Shakers repudiated marriage, regarding sexual relations as expressions of lust, and they lived apart as brothers and sisters in dormitories. Increase in their number was attained through conversions and the adoption of orphaned children. The Shakers rejected not only private property, but liquor, meat, ornaments, and voting. They had no interest in literature, learning, or amusements. Hard work was a sanctifying influence, and they were excellent farmers, builders, cabinetmakers, seedsmen, seamstresses, and medicine compounders. They had no trouble earning their sustenance. Their plain and pleasingly proportioned furniture brings high prices today from antique collectors. Other Americans regarded them with curiosity and occasionally with envy. By 1810 the value of community living and shared property was emphasized over theology to attract members, but it was not enough.

The Indiana community embraced 1,300 acres, and by 1811 counted 300 members, 131 of them children. Tecumseh found no fault with them, but after the Battle of Tippecanoe and the declaration of war, they became fearful of their safety. Yet, being pacifists, they did not want to build even a defensive stockade. Instead, they departed for Kentucky, where some of them settled at South Union, a few miles below Bowling Green, and others established Pleasant Hill, near Harrodsburg. As danger passed, many of them returned to Busseron Creek in 1814. By 1823 there were 200 Shakers living at West Union. Malaria infected them each summer, and in 1827 they pulled out for good. Vincennes bid them an affectionate farewell as they returned both to Kentucky and to Ohio. Their buildings at West Union were ultimately razed, so that no trace remains in the state.

Several years before the Shakers left, a second religious community that later became New Harmony, mentioned earlier, was established on the Wabash by a group of German millennialists from Harmonie in western Pennsylvania. They called their Indiana location Harmonie—or Harmony—also. Basically Separatists, they had no name, but were called Harmonists, or "Rappites," since they were followers of George Rapp (1770–1847), a self-made preacher of incredible self-righteousness and autocracy. In his native Wurttemberg, Rapp had been originally a member of the official Evangelical church. He separated from it in 1785, under the conviction that he was a prophet, and began preaching in his own house. He assured his listeners that Christ would return in his, Rapp's, lifetime and begin a reign of a thousand peaceful years on earth. His doctrine gathered appeal as the Napoleonic wars began. When Rapp was forbidden to hold meetings, he decided to migrate. From the reference in the Book of Revelations about the Sunwoman, who fled into the wilderness to escape evil, he had developed ideas about how the Second Coming should be awaited: his followers should find a new, untrammeled location; private property, including the fruits of one's labor, should be surrendered to common ownership—actually to Rapp, who would provide food, clothing, and shelter to the members, as well as providing all the religious instruction and rules of conduct they would need. Celibacy was recommended, although Rapp had a wife and two children; no more marriages were approved, but married couples could live together if they produced no more children.

Rapp came to America in 1803 and bought land in Butler County, Pennsylvania. Tall, robust, blue-eyed and bearded, he had impressed his authority on several hundred neighbors, who followed him to people the new community. Good farmers and careful managers, they prospered. Perhaps the smartest step taken by Father Rapp, as he was called, was to adopt an astute young man as his son and his business manager. This Frederick Rapp saw to it that the Harmonie Society made money and saved it. Vine-growing was their special talent, and the cold of western Pennsylvania limited it. Also, worldy temptations were coming too close. The Rapps sought more land in a greater wilderness and a warmer clime. Exploring down the Ohio River, they turned up the Wabash in Indiana Territory's Posey County and bought nearly 25,000 acres from the government for $61,000. They sold their old tract for $100,000. The new migration began in 1815, and more than five hundred of the pious and patient Germans laid out and built a new community, again called Harmonie—or Harmony.

Four dormitories, two for men and two for women, were constructed to make celibacy easier. Each had a kitchen and a common room. Couples and families were allowed private houses, and the best one was Father Rapp's. The houses were not all equal: forty two-story dwellings of brick and frame stuck out amid eighty-six log cabins. Two granaries, two sawmills, two distilleries, and a brewery were joined by a textile mill, a dyehouse, and a hemp and oil mill. In European fashion, the fields and vineyards were outside of town, although each house might have a kitchen garden and a stable. They built solidly, plainly, and well. They fed cattle and sheep and cultivated orchards. The sawmills cut timbers for the houses in standard sizes and numbered them, introducing the modular dwelling of interchangeable parts. Regular streets were designated. Farm produce, whiskey, woolens, rope, hats, and leathers were shipped to New Orleans, and again the community prospered. Directly from Wurttemberg came 130 new converts in 1817; Rapp did not proselyte in this country. They all led a quiet and profoundly regulated life, apparently without complaint and largely without defections. A visitor in 1822 learned that very few could speak English, nor would they answer questions. He found them self-sufficient and not spending their sales revenues on anything. He never saw one of them laugh, and the whole town was unnaturally still.

Another visitor declared that worship service took place three times a day; more likely, services were limited to Sundays and Thursdays. In a large central garden was a curious labyrinth of hedges whose intricacies illustrated something of their theology. In 1823 they were building a huge brick church (their second) in the form of a cross. They used instrumental music in their service, and sometimes a band played for reapers in the harvest season. What Rapp did with all their income was a mystery to every visitor, since nothing seemed to be purchased. The mystery was not lessened when Rapp abruptly sold the whole town in 1825 to Robert Owen for a different kind of community, which dispensed with religion. The Rappites returned to western Pennsylvania and established another community called Economy, where George Rapp died, certain to the end that he would not go before greeting a returned Christ.

Thus, before 1830, both Shakers and Rappites had passed from the Hoosier scene. The two communities were laboratory demonstrations of what Christianity did not mean to most Americans. Since long before the Revolution, human rights had rested on property rights, and deliberately to sacrifice one's property in the quest for salvation seemed, to Hoosiers, a shed-

INDIANA

A photographer's essay by Joe Clark, H.B.S.S.

Photographs in sequence

Corn.
Lockerbie Square, Indianapolis.
University Square Memorial Park, Indianapolis.
Courthouse, Lafayette.
Steel mill, Gary.
Boys with bicycles, Gary.
Men on Ohio Street, Gary.
Amish man and boys with buggies, Shipshewana.
Main Street storefronts, Vincennes.
Farm near Shipshewana.
Lake Michigan and steel mill at Gary.
Horses in field, Brown County.
Cornfield and bins south of Lafayette.
Roadside market on Route 135 near Beanblossom.
Bridge and canoe, Fort Wayne.

ding of responsibility and counterproductive. The challenge of religion to them was rather to live in God's world as an individual or as a family, to cope with all one's problems, view them as tests of faith, and carry on a Christian commitment.

More to their liking were inspiring evangelical revivals, because they appealed to people as individuals. They were the principle means by which the Christian church as a mission could reach the scattered frontiersmen. One such revival was carefully described by Frances Trollope, an Englishwoman managing a farm near Cincinnati. With a friend, Mrs. Trollope attended a camp meeting somewhere in the backwoods of Indiana in 1829, undoubtedly in the southeast sector. They arrived at night, after the preaching had ceased, and found the people scattered in their light tents or walking around the grounds, praying, preaching, singing, and lamenting. Mrs. Trollope records the emotionally charged scene vividly. Lifting the flap of one tent, she and her friend saw about thirty persons kneeling in a circle on the straw-covered flooring. One young man and the distraught young girl beside him fell on their faces in the straw before the vehemence of the gaunt preacher fulminating and gesturing violently in the center of the tent. Others in the circle sobbed and groaned and called unceasingly "on the name of Jesus." At midnight, some two thousand persons were drawn by the sound of a horn from similar scenes to another general exhortation, which lasted until dawn. The worshippers, exhibiting intense emotional distress, were goaded ceaselessly by the objurgations of several preachers circulating among them, assuring them of "the enormous depravity of man . . . and of his perfect sanctification after he had wrestled sufficiently with the Lord to get hold of him." Amid mounting tension and stress, the preachers invited anxious sinners forward to "wrestle with the Lord," and many, "uttering howlings and groans so terrible that I shall never cease to shudder when I recall them . . . appeared to drag each other forward . . . soon all lying on the ground in an indescribable confusion . . . incessant and violent motion . . . Hysterical sobbings, convulsive groans, shrieks and screams . . . burst forth." Mrs. Trollope was especially concerned about the number of attractive and impressionable young girls whom the preachers seemed to single out for special attention, "at once exciting and soothing their groans. I heard the muttered 'Sister! dear sister!' I saw the insidious lips approach the cheeks of the unhappy girls . . . breathing into their ears consolations that tinged the pale cheek with red." The service broke up at dawn, and the worshippers set about preparing and eating substantial breakfasts, as heartily "as if the night had been spent in dancing; and I marked many a fair but pale face that I recognized as a demoniac of the night . . . beside a swain, to whom she carefully administered hot coffee and eggs." [2]

Yet even that kind of wholesale fervor and exhibitionism lost its appeal. Indiana escaped the frequent camp meetings so popular in Kentucky and Tennessee. Hoosiers of religious bent preferred to stick with the established denominations and identify themselves with the familiar churches that recognized a secular life of family units, private property, and dignified ritual.

By 1830, when state population had reached a figure of 345,000, there were in Indiana probably 20,000 Catholics, according to the state historian of that church. Their centers were Vincennes, Fort Wayne, and South Bend. Under the bishop of Baltimore since 1789, Indiana in 1830 was assigned to a new diocese—Bardstown, Kentucky—and then in 1834 the diocese of Vincennes was established to include all of Indiana and the eastern third of Illinois.

In 1832, membership in the Methodist church reached 20,000 also, and a separate Indiana Conference was organized. Only eight years later, Methodist church membership jumped to 52,600. The rigors of circuit riding caused young ministers to agree to forego marriage for a time. After four years on the circuit, they might marry if they obtained permission from their elders. One young woman of evident piety and personality at-

2. Frances Trollope, *Domestic Manners of the Americans* (London: Printed for Whittaker, Treacher and Co., 1832), pp. 139–145.

tracted the attention of three bachelor ministers, each of whom
sought permission from the same presiding elder to propose to
Cora. Each one attested that the Lord had guided him in his
choice. The puzzled elder could only conclude: "Somebody
must have misunderstood the Lord." [3] Whether the ineffable
Cora received three proposals, or one—or none—is left in mystery.

Baptists reached a total of 11,300 in 1833. Despite several
divisions in their denomination, they were united in favor of
complete separation of church and state. Unlike their other Protestant colleagues, they did not believe in missions, and that
tenet retarded their growth. In addition, they did not support
public education and did not require an educated clergy. Inspira-
tion was enough.

The Presbyterians increased slowly, achieving about 5,000
members in 1837. They did not make much use of itinerant
preachers, but settled their ministers in churches. They established Hanover College in 1827 and Wabash College in
1833.

All three of these major Protestant denominations were ac-
tively opposed to slavery, drinking, and gambling. Defections
from all three denominations permitted the rise of the Christian
Church or Disciples of Christ in the 1830s. With the appearance
of Germans, Lutheran churches multiplied in the 1840s.
Quakers, especially those from North Carolina, flowed into the
upper Whitewater valley and were influential by the time of
statehood in 1816. They grew to 26,000 in 1890 and have
increased only about 10 percent since then.

Just above Batesville, German Catholics settled in 1837 at
Oldenburg. It was completely a religious community, without
industries. The Church of the Holy Family now occupies an imposing brick building erected in 1861 and 1862. Next to it is a
Franciscan monastery where candidates for the priesthood re-

3. William Warren Sweet, *Circuit-Rider Days in Indiana* (Indianapolis: W. K. Stew-
art Co., 1916), pp. 55–56.

ceive their final education. Across the street is the Convent of the Immaculate Conception, the mother home of the Sisters of St. Francis.

At the same time, German catholics also flowed into Jasper and made their language the prevailing one until World War I. These people came directly from Germany at the instigation of a German priest of persuasive power. The hills and forests he saw in southern Indiana reminded him of home, where many of the artisans were woodworkers. He assured them that they would find a familiar setting in Dubois County. In 1976 Jasper was about 65 percent Catholic, down from 85 percent; Huntingburg was about 50 percent Catholic. Jasper contained twenty-four woodworking plants, where unions were weak because the immigrants invested in the factories that gave them employment.

South of the county seat, St. Meinrad was founded in 1854 to house a Benedictine archabbey that grew virtually self-sufficient through farming and crafts. It supported a seminary for training priests in the Order of St. Benedict and a large church famous for its resonant organ and Gregorian choir. A few miles west was another German Catholic community, Ferdinand, known for its Benedictine Convent of the Immaculate Conception.

The 1850 census showed more than 2,400 churches in Indiana, for a population of a million. The Methodists accounted for 795 churches, the various Baptist sects for 770, the Presbyterians for 295, and the Christians for 193. The Friends had 91, the Catholics 69, the Lutherans 59, and the United Brethren 59.[4] Altogether, there was one church for every 530 persons, Kentucky had one for every 540. Religious Massachusetts had one for every 702 inhabitants. Indiana seemed indeed to be a religious state, and at mid-century it was overwhelmingly Protestant.

Mennonites came directly from Switzerland in 1835 and settled first in Adams County in the north, then spread westward. They were farmers and craftsmen. The Amish (the conservative wing of the Mennonites which had separated about 1700); mi-

4. Thornbrough and Riker, *Readings in Indiana History,* pp. 477–478.

grated from Pennsylvania to Elkhart County in 1840, leaving small communities in northern Ohio. In 1971 the Mennonites in Indiana numbered only 37,800, but they maintained churches and supported Goshen College and a publishing house. In contrast, the Amish, visually distinguished by their plain dress, beards, broad-brimmed hats and bonnets, and known for their rejection of electricity, telephones, and automobiles, were opposed to education beyond the eighth grade and worshipped in the homes of their members every *other* Sunday. They numbered fewer than 5,000 in 1971.

Jews migrated to Indiana in small numbers after about 1820. They were peddlers, merchants, tradesmen, and occasionally farmers. Moving down the Ohio from Cincinnati, they settled in the river towns from Lawrenceburg to Mount Vernon, and turned up the Wabash. As ten Jewish males more than twelve years of age were required to form a *minyan,* or congregation, there was no group large enough until a Fort Wayne congregation emerged in 1848. It was followed by another congregation at Lafayette the next year, at Indianapolis in 1856, and at Evansville in 1857. These were conservative congregations, as the reform Jews were not organized until later. In the 1880s Jews from eastern Europe began to arrive and establish orthodox synagogues, and a few of the older congregations then began to associate with the reform branch. The 1890 census showed only 3,600 Jews in the state. By the advent of World War I, that number had risen to 25,800, a figure that remained fairly constant for nearly sixty years. In 1974 Jews totaled 26,200 or .5 percent of the state's population. Although most of them have a sympathetic interest in the safety and prosperity of Israel, they are as proudly Hoosier as any other Hoosier.

After the Civil War, Catholic churches became increasingly urban. A latent anti-Catholic prejudice among Protestants was intensified when Catholic leaders sought in 1869 public support of parochial schools and objected to readings from the King James Version of the Bible in public schools. The high-riding Republican party complained that Catholics were Democrats. Yet they suffered no overt hostility and by 1916 were the largest denomination in the state, with 272,000 communicants. Italian and Slavic immigrants added to the Catholic variety, while the original French element almost disappeared. *Our Sunday Visitor,* established at Huntington in 1912, grew to become one of the most influential Catholic periodicals in the country.

Concommitant with the growth of cities and the development of the automobile early in the twentieth century came a broad decline in the number of rural Protestant churches. Barely able to support even a part-time pastor in times of limited travel, they were abandoned by a declining rural population in an age of growing mobility. The churches were no longer social centers for their areas. Some of them had been established only by the separatist tendencies of quarrelsome members and were too small to survive.

Neither Negro population nor the foreign-born had increased in numbers enough in 1880 to draw the attention of a peculiar vigilantism that rose in Indiana. It was another type of moral force, nonpolitical, nonracial, and nonforeign. "Regulators" formed early in the state. A company of them near Vincennes broke up a gang of counterfeiters and robbers in the early 1820s. An 1852 law allowing irregular enforcement of laws against "horse thieves and other felons" encouraged vigilantes in the thinly settled counties of the north. After the Civil War they took on the clandestine punishment of individuals who deviated from the local moral code, on the ground that they were protecting the young from degrading influences.

The state as a whole had moved ahead of the southern Indiana hill country that railroads did not cross, where manufacturing did not prosper, farming was marginal, and schools as well as roads were neglected. From 1873 to 1893, "Whitecaps"—so named for the hood they wore to hide their identities—flourished in eight southern rural counties. Residents there tended to judge others on personal qualities: how honest they were in dealings, how sober and industrious and religious they were, how they treated their families, and so on. Whitecaps were concerned with such domestic sins as cruelty to children, wife-beating, drunkenness, gambling, infidelity, even laziness.

They believed that they were sustaining the fabric of rural society. Members were sworn to secrecy, loyalty to their fellows, and absolute obedience to their leader. They performed their missions on horseback at night. The victim selected for correction or exile was first given a warning to mend his ways or to leave. If there was no change, he was visited by a masked band who whipped him, and one person was designated to publicize that punishment locally. If any attacker could be identified and the victim brought suit, the jury would be composed of fellow Whitecaps who rendered a verdict of acquittal or disagreement. Members also provided alibis for one another. A web of corruption was spun. The governor threatened sheriffs and county prosecutors in flagrant cases, without result because he faced the American predilection to enforce morality individually rather than through judicial institutions. Whippings began to give way to greater violence, and victims were killed with impunity. Social sins occasionally yielded to personal vendettas.

After a *New York Times* reporter visited southern Indiana in 1887 and wrote about the lawlessness observed, Governor Isaac Gray instructed the attorney general to clean out the Whitecaps. The attorney general was unsuccessful, but the general assembly did pass a law against wearing masks. What finally destroyed the movement was a peculiar occurrence in Harrison County in August 1893.

A family named Conrad (pronounced *Coon-rod*), living on a remote farm, consisted of a widow, two sons, and an unmarried daughter with a child. The husband had been murdered in the spring, and the two sons, suspected of the murder, were hauled before a grand jury, but charges were dismissed. Nevertheless, the community believed that the boys had killed their father. Their mother did not. Later, the sons found their two dogs poisoned. Then they received a warning to leave the county. Instead, the boys bought buckshot for their four shotguns and waited each night for the Whitecaps to come. One Saturday night, more than forty hooded men rode into the farmyard after dark. The boys were out in the bushes, so the two women were taken out in the yard and threatened. A noose was prepared for

Mrs. Conrad. Then one of the Whitecaps lighted a lantern. That was all the boys needed. They shot into the mob, quickly changed position to avoid the return fire, and with their second guns they fired again. Three of the Whitecaps lay expiring, others were wounded. The troop mounted and rode off, leaving five behind. Three men died at once, and the other two lingered till morning. Three more were believed wounded. The community was shocked by the loss of five prominent citizens, and their funerals drew hundreds. Meanwhile, the Conrad family crossed the Ohio into Kentucky. The boys were indeed innocent of killing their father: some thirty years later, the true murderer of Mr. Conrad confessed on his death bed.[5]

The aftereffects of the shooting at the Conrad farm were unexpected. Indianapolis and Chicago newspapers upheld the Conrads and derided the lawless Whitecaps. More important was the immediate local reaction. After all the pledges of standing together, the group had abandoned five of its own men, two of whom might have lived if they had been taken to a physician. If they couldn't rely on one another, who would risk participation in a subsequent raid? Whitecapping came to an abrupt end. A final incident in Monroe County in 1911 prompted Governor Thomas R. Marshall to prosecute and convict two suspects. The atmosphere had changed.

Toward the end of the nineteenth century, a few liberal Protestants in urban centers turned to the "social gospel" aimed at improving the condition of the factory workers rather than the saving of souls. The most influential ministers were the Reverend Oscar C. McCulloch, a Congregationalist in Indianapolis, active from 1877 until his death in 1891, and the Reverend Worth M. Tippy, a Methodist active in Terre Haute and Indianapolis until he removed to Cleveland in 1905. Their efforts were stirred by the growing gulf between organized religion and organized labor. However, most clergymen managed to ignore

5. Madeleine E. Noble, "The White Caps of Harrison and Crawford County, Indiana: A Study in the Violent Enforcement of Morality" (Ph.D. diss., University of Michigan, 1973).

that challenge. What they found difficult was to appeal to factory workers and avoid endorsing unions, socialism, or other industrial reforms that seemed alien to church concerns. The Baptists did create a committee on social service whose report in 1914 was a strong indictment of the "present world system of capitalistic competition," but it was not sustained.

In contravention of all that McCulloch and Tippy stood for, new churches of holiness and pentecostal orientation appeared, with their emphasis on individual salvation. The most important of these in Indiana was the Church of God, which had opened its first church in 1881 at Beaver Dam under the aegis of Daniel Warner, who had also started a religious journal called the *Gospel Trumpet* at Rome City. The journal was moved in 1906 to Anderson, which became the headquarters of the new denomination. In a similar mood, the majority of German Protestants affiliated with the conservative Missouri Synod of the Lutheran church.

The churches of Indiana continued to grow, but never became known as a liberalizing force, in theology, in education, or on the issues of welfare, discrimination, or abortion. As the twentieth century wore on, they attacked immorality and the liquor interest, but with rare exceptions they did not fight the Ku Klux Klan when it festered in Indiana. Within each denomination there are churches that strongly support the Indiana Council of Churches, and those that remain suspicious of and opposed to that organization with its national and international affiliations. Yet if it has seemed that Indiana churches were self-absorbed and isolationist, that was not a true picture, either. A few sects have been conspicuous leaders in international outreach.

The Quakers have supported their Friends Service Committee, which has carried relief and instruction all over the world. The Church of the Brethren sponsored relief work in Spain after that country's civil war. It was a Brethren agent, Dan West of Goshen, who conceived of the Heifer Project in 1944, aimed at reestablishing herds in war-ravaged countries. He collected donated livestock, raised money for shipping them to a port, and asked the recipient country to pay the final shipping charges.

The first offspring of a donated animal had to be given to another family, but after that all of the new-born animals might be
kept by the original recipient. Cows, bulls, goats, sheep, hogs,
and rabbits have been exported. In 1952 the project sent three
planes, each loaded with 72,000 eggs, directly from Indiana to
Korea to revive the poultry-and-egg industry. Today, more than
half the chickens in Korea are of Hoosier descent. Don't speak
to Koreans about Hoosiers being self-centered isolationists.

The Mennonites joined the Heifer Project, and gradually a
dozen other major denominations supported it. Their representatives form a board of directors. By 1971 they had shipped
animals and agricultural equipment to ninety foreign countries
and even to several of our own southern states. Mr. West retired, and headquarters of the project was moved to a farm near
Little Rock, Arkansas, but the Midwest Regional Office is
maintained at Goshen. There is also an eastern regional office in
Massachusetts, and a western one in California. The work continued in the 1970s and was one U.S. relief program that
foreign governments did not criticize.

More than 800 Cuban refugees were relocated and accepted
in the state after they fled the Castro regime. In 1976 teams of
Indiana Seventh Day Adventists helped build houses in Gua-
temala for victims of the recent earthquake. In Nappanee the
Church of the Brethren established a sales outlet for the products of craftsmen in the West Indies, where their missionaries
labor. All that is a record any state could be proud of, and it
was initiated by the smaller and less fashionable denominations.

The last census of church membership, made in 1971,
showed that, nationally, 49.6 percent of the total population
belonged to a church. Indiana fell below this average: 44.6 percent of all Indianans were members. Michigan and Ohio showed
a bit more, but Kentucky, Illinois, and Wisconsin were well
above the national average. Nevertheless, some Hoosiers still
regard themselves as living in a state of church-goers.

At that time, the Catholic church had the largest registry in
Indiana, with almost 14 percent of the state's church membership gathered into 513 churches, though the Catholic church

counts children as church members, which Protestant churches do not. This percentage is much less than that of Roman Catholics in surrounding states, except for Kentucky, where the percentage is below Indiana's. The largest concentration of Catholics (not the greatest number) was found in Dubois, Perry, Franklin, Ripley, Martin, and Spencer counties, all in southern Indiana, which is heavily populated by descendants of German Catholics.

Methodists were second, with 8 percent of the church memberships. Lutherans were third, with 3.4 percent, Christians were fourth with 3 percent, followed closely by the Baptists, with 2.9 percent, and the Presbyterians, with 2.5 percent. With 6,092 recognized churches, Indiana had for its population one church for every 852 persons, a decided decrease in proportion since 1850.

The state remains preponderantly Protestant, and an uncertain portion is conservative. Anderson is the world headquarters for the Church of God and maintains a denominational college there. Up at Winona Lake, the Billy Sunday tradition of evangelism is carried on with successive conferences of evangelical pastors and laymen in the summer, and a seminary, Grace Bible College, that operates in other seasons. The Youth for Christ movement was started in Indianapolis in 1943 and joined with an international organization the following year.

In summer, vacation Bible schools for children flourish. Conferences of pastors and elders are held at resort hotels or assembly grounds. The southern heritage shows up in gospel trios and quartets, which seem to appear everywhere at once, making up in sincerity and fervor what they lack in musical talent. Church affiliation is respected throughout the state. No one denigrates it, no one apologizes for it.

Whether or not the work of the churches may be credited, respect for law prevails generally. Crime has not prospered here. Back in 1824, ruffians of all sorts received a rude shock. After a gang of five white men slaughtered a party of nine Indians near modern Pendleton, a posse went after them and captured four of the murderers. They were tried and sentenced to be hanged, at a time when killing Indians was rarely considered a crime. Three of the men were promptly executed, but the fourth and youngest was reprieved at the last moment. In 1868 three Reno brothers from Seymour and a fourth companion were jailed at New Albany for train robbery near Seymour. The depredation was their second; they had the dubious distinction of conducting the first train robbery in the country in 1866. One hundred scarlet-hooded men boarded the train from Seymour to New Albany, overpowered the sheriff, took the four men out of jail, and hanged them. In 1886 the four Archer brothers met a similar fate at Shoals, after a particularly brutal murder. The last lynching in the state was of two Negroes in Marion, accused of rape and murder in 1930. Law enforcement was strengthened by the organization of state police in 1921.

Modern Indiana has a lower crime rate than most of its neighbors. In 1975 the state suffered 260,847 crimes, or 4,911 per 100,000 population; 17,677 of them were violent crimes, or 333 per 100,000; the rest were property crimes. Illinois showed 5,382 crimes per 100,000, and almost twice as many violent crimes as Indiana. Michigan had 6,800 crimes per 100,000 and more than twice as many violent crimes. Ohio showed the same overall rate of 4,914 crimes per 100,000 population, but violent crimes there were higher at 408 per 100,000. Kentucky was lower in both categories.

As for urban crime, Indianapolis suffered 95 murders in 1975, an increase from the year before. Gary had 77, Evansville and Fort Wayne 14 each, South Bend and East Chicago, 13 each. In other states, Louisville counted 74 murders, Cincinnati 64, Cleveland 288, St. Louis 240, Detroit 633, and Chicago 818. One further difference is that criminal gangs and rackets warfare did not develop in Indianapolis in the 1920s and 1930s, as they did in Chicago, Detroit, and St. Louis. Indiana's most famous criminal, John Dillinger, was a lone bank robber. Some St. Louis mobsters are supposed to have infiltrated Terre Haute for a short period of rum-running between stills in southern Indiana and Chicago. Gambling rings in Indianapolis, Gary, and Terre Haute have been broken. If Indiana did not escape the social effects of the twentieth century, it came off better in the incidence of crime than most of its neighbors.

Indiana had an opportunity to develop as good an educational system as Ohio or Michigan, but neglected it. Indeed, with the examples provided by New Harmony, it could have assumed a position of leadership. A portent of good things to come had been signaled in the organization of a circulating library in Vincennes in 1806. The Literary Society of Vevay was founded in 1814, and a theatrical society of young men in Vincennes. A Masonic Lodge had been chartered in 1809 in Vincennes. But the state failed to live up to its potential. In brief, its provision for public schooling was nothing short of disgraceful. As a result, it suffered immoderate illiteracy, persistence of prejudices, industrial lagging, and political primitivism until recent times.

The Ordinance of 1787 had admonished that "Religion, morality, and knowledge being necessary to good government and the happiness of mankind, schools and the means of education shall forever be encouraged," and public land had been provided for financing public schools by its sale. Further, the first Indiana constitution, in 1816, had virtuously declared that "It shall be the duty of the General assembly, as soon as circumstances will permit, to provide by law for a general system of education, ascending in regular gradation, from township schools to a state university, wherein tuition shall be gratis, and equally open to all." [6] Yet the saving clause, "as soon as circumstances will permit," was used as an excuse for delay and inaction.

Successive governors called the assembly's attention to this section, but could not prod that body into a decision. The Reverend Isaac Reed wrote in 1827: "The common schools are generally of a low character when compared with the schools of the Northern States. Here and there is found a district where the school is well supported and well taught. The schools are nearly

6. Indiana, *Constitution* (1816).

all taught by men. There are many people of common school education, but there are also many men and many women who cannot read at all.'' [7]

The first historian of Indiana, John B. Dillon, published an eloquent plea in his Logansport newspaper in 1836. His figures of speech tumbled out in mixed images:

> If the time shall ever come when this mighty fabric shall totter; when the beacon of joy that now rises in pillar of fire, a sign and wonder of the world, shall wax dim, the cause will be found in the ignorance of the people. If our union is still to continue to cheer the hopes and animate the efforts of the oppressed of every nation; if our fields are to be untrod by the hirelings of despotism; if long days of blessedness are to attend our country in her career of glory; if you would have the sun continue to shed his unclouded rays upon the face of freeman, then EDUCATE ALL THE CHILDREN OF THE LAND. This alone startles the tyrant in his dreams of power, and rouses the slumbering energies of an oppressed people. It was intelligence that reared up the majestic columns of national glory; and this and sound morality alone can prevent their crumbling to ashes. [8]

Then Caleb Mills, a graduate of Dartmouth College (1828) and of Andover Theological Seminary, came to Indiana as first instructor at Wabash College in 1833. He was shocked at what he found in the poor elementary schools and the only occasional secondary schools. Colleges would never prosper, he believed, until there were adequate high schools to provide graduates with a proper academic background. Further, he saw that high schools would not flourish until elementary education was widespread and highly prized.

Yet, the state continued languidly to rely on private efforts. The general attitude was that parents could teach reading, writing, and arithmetic to their children, or neighboring families could band together and hire a teacher for three or four months, or churches could open elementary schools as well as they could

7. Quoted in Lindley, *Indiana as Seen by Early Travelers,* p. 501.
8. *Logansport Canal Telegraph,* November 19, 1836.

found colleges. Such schools had to charge tuition, of course. The large proportion of Indianans who had come from southern states lacked a tradition of state-supported education; and more pressing matters made schools appear to be luxuries. Only gradually were township trustees allowed to build and maintain schools if local parents would suffer a tax for support. Two depressions, in 1819–1820 and 1837–1840, were good excuses for delay. Further, the priority given internal improvements—which did not include schools, yet became so costly that the state defaulted on their improvement bonds—discouraged every attempt at a statewide system of education. When the sale of the townships granted by Congress (to provide for support of schools) did not produce enough money to operate schools, the assembly was unwilling to set a tax to supplement that support. Curiously, neither Catholics nor the stronger Protestant sects wanted nonsectarian schools, for fear of weakening Christian faith.

The only bright spot, and it was little more than a candle, was in New Harmony. There an enlightened adult community insisted on an advanced school system. Educational theory was linked to the social reform Robert Owen expected—and failed—to demonstrate in his Indiana laboratory. The doctrines of Pestalozzi and von Fellenberg in Switzerland had converted William Maclure, a rich Scotsman, who moved to Philadelphia in 1796. He imported one of Pestalozzi's colleagues, Joseph Neef, and two teachers trained in the master's methods: Madame Marie Fretageot and William Phiquepal d'Arusmont. All of them became excited by Owen's model community and migrated to New Harmony in January 1826 to inaugurate a new kind of schooling.

In brief, the Pestalozzian system was intensely vocational in an age of classical learning. It was a method of diffusing useful knowledge by means of instruction combined with manual labor. Further, instruction was to involve objects presented to class attention, rather than names or concepts. The pace of schooling was geared to the child's desire to learn, and he was never to be punished. Older students were drafted to help younger ones under a teacher's supervision. As Maclure saw it, education was governed by its social purpose. It began with the very young (here was the first free kindergarten in the country) and continued with adult education for life. Colleges, he thought, served only the children of the idle and nonproductive; their funds should be channeled to elementary schools as the only ones really entitled to government support. As an adjunct, Maclure created a Workingman's Institute as a library and cultural center, and he bequeathed his fortune to founding more of them. But the advantages enjoyed by New Harmony children were not duplicated elsewhere in the state.

In 1976 New Harmony was being restored, under joint auspices and without an exclusive focus. Some Rappite buildings are being renovated, the Owenite "scientific period" of intellectual prominence between 1825 and the Civil War will be exploited, and store fronts are being remodeled as of an earlier day. The state was represented by the old New Harmony Commission, which owns a few properties, and the Division of Natural Resources, which is developing a state park on the river. The commission formed Historic New Harmony, Incorporated, to receive a substantial grant from Lilly Endowment for acquiring more properties and restoring them, for educational programs, and for store-front remodeling. Both groups work closely with Mrs. Kenneth Owen of Texas and New Harmony. The owner of several historic houses and some operating businesses, Mrs. Owen erected a roofless church, a motel, and a youth hostel. The concerted aim is to establish more than a living museum, to bring about a restoration of New Harmony's reputation for cultural leadership through a steady program of interpreted structures, college extension classes, scholarly conferences, public lectures, concerts, and plays. Cheap commercialization has been zoned out, and several attractive new shops have opened. The town still has only a thousand inhabitants, but two hundred new jobs will be created. Not everyone is happy over the anticipated influx of visitors or the tripling of real estate prices that has already come about, as they will be felt in the next round of tax assessments. But the alternative to historical exploitation was deterioration and stagnation.

For six years, starting late in 1846, Caleb Mills, then president of Wabash College, issued annual exhortations to Hoosiers on the vital importance of public schools, hoping to shame them into action. His messages were headed impatiently, "Read, Discuss and Circulate." Several county seminaries charging tuition were established for secondary education, but they were usually short-lived; those academies supported by churches were more numerous and fared better. The quality of elementary schooling varied widely from place to place. A missionary-minded New Englander through and through, Mills was eloquent and persistent; he aroused parents, and he made some legislators squirm. His main accomplishment was that, as preparations began for a new constitutional convention to meet in 1851, it became increasingly clear that a new obligation toward public education would be assumed and defined in the charter.

Attempts at creating a university were at first equally feeble, which is all the more surprising in view of the insight shown by an early territorial legislature. In the act of November 29, 1806, to create a university, the preamble reads:

Whereas the independence, happiness, and energy of every republic depends (under the influence of the destinies of Heaven) upon the wisdom, virtue, talents, and energy of its citizens and rulers; and whereas science, literature, and the liberal arts contribute in an eminent degree to improve those qualities and acquirements; and whereas learning hath ever been found the ablest advocate of genuine liberty, the best supporter of rational religion, and the source of the only solid and imperishable glory which nations can acquire; and forasmuch as literature and philosophy furnish the most useful and pleasing occupations, improving and varying the enjoyments of prosperity, affording relief under the pressure of misfortune, and hope and consolation in the hour of death; and considering that in a commonwealth where the humblest citizen may be elected to highest public offices, and where the heaven-born prerogative of the right to elect and reject is retained and secured to the citizens, the knowledge which is requisite for a magistrate and elector should be widely diffused.[9]

This noble declaration amplified the preamble of the Northwest Ordinance. It is not succinct, and it was not expressed in the most felicitous manner, yet it rings. In it is an astonishing rejection of vocational training (when frontier conditions emphasized practical know-how) in favor, not of a classical curriculum, but simply of literature and philosophy because they are actually and truly useful in all vocations as well as stimulating to a questing mind.

This same territorial legislature incorporated Vincennes University, which opened in 1810 and struggled along for fifteen years, when it lapsed into a county seminary for a time. Meanwhile, the state assembly created, in 1820, a state seminary at Bloomington, which opened in 1825 and three years later became Indiana College, with sixty students and the redoubtable Andrew Wylie (1789–1851) as president. Wylie was a Presbyterian minister and later an Episcopal priest, and he was a tolerant and patient man. Baccalaureate degrees were awarded to four students in 1831. Hanover College and Wabash College began giving degrees in 1834 and 1838. The Methodists founded Asbury University (De Pauw) in 1837 at Greencastle, and in the same year the Baptists opened a Manual Labor Institute that became Franklin College. The fathers of the Congregation of the Holy Cross started the University of Notre Dame in 1842, near South Bend. If they all neglected history, economics, modern languages, and literature at first, they were strong in Latin, Greek, classical literature, mathematics, physics, astronomy, and philosophy or religion. Education in Indiana quickly became top-heavy, an inverted pyramid: colleges were ample for those qualified to attend, but few students were

9. *The Laws of Indiana Territory, 1801–1809*, edited by Francis S. Philbrick, Illinois Historical Collections 21 (1930; reprint edition, Indianapolis: Indiana Historical Bureau, 1931).

prepared by secondary schooling, and some escaped instruction entirely.

Under the circumstances, it was inevitable that illiteracy should rear its empty head. In 1840, one in seven white persons over the age of twenty could not read or write. Ten years later, illiterates composed one-fifth of the adult population, and Indiana ranked twenty-third among the twenty-six states in literacy. It stood lower than all but three of the slave states; all other northern states were above it. Anticipating that statistic, Caleb Mills warned the general assembly in 1847 that "we are the most ignorant of the *free states. . . .* Some of our counties are enveloped in a thicker intellectual darkness than shrouds *any state* in the Union." [10] As much as any other factor, that ignorance sustained the Hoosier image noticed by outsiders. The public schooling that might have reduced that dubious distinction and ironed out regional differences among state citizens was simply not available.

The new constitution of 1851 accepted state responsibility for free public schools. However, although in that charter the county seminaries were abolished and higher education was conspicuously neglected, Article 8 made it incumbent on the assembly "to provide by law for a general and uniform system of Common Schools, wherein tuition shall be without charge, and equally open to all." [11] A state superintendent of education was to be elected. The assembly was also required to provide for the care and education of the blind and the deaf and dumb. Provision for schools "equally open to all" was qualified by a prohibition against the children of resident people of color: they could not attend any public schools even if they paid a tuition, and their property was not to be taxed for school purposes. It was a harsh, indefensible exclusion.

Townships could levy taxes for schools, and so could towns

---

10. C. W. Moores, "Caleb Mills and the Indiana School System," in *Indiana Historical Society Publications* 3 (1905): 6, 437.

11. Indiana, *Constitution* (1851), Art. 8.

and cities. Nevertheless, suits were brought to outlaw such taxes, and the state supreme court ruled in 1854 that local levies for tuition (not buildings) violated the constitutional prohibition against local or special laws. Thus, when the way for advancement seemed cleared, some schools had to close for a few years, until a more enlightened court in 1867 decided in favor of school taxes, and not just for buildings. Even so, during the first five years of the new law, 1852–1857, more than 2,700 schoolhouses were built. Moreover, the first publicly supported high school in the West for both boys and girls opened at Indianapolis in 1853. About half of the incorporated towns reporting in 1856 had school systems. Again, the results were seen first in rising literacy: only one in every nine adults was illiterate in 1860—a gross total less than in 1850, amid a larger population. The ground was laid at long last for expansion of free public schools after the Civil War.

The new trends were toward lengthening the school year to nine months, broadening the curriculum, raising the educational requirements of teachers and providing a normal school at Terre Haute in 1870 for their training, and increasing the supervision by county and state officials. Attendance for children between eight and fourteen years of age was finally made compulsory in 1897. In secondary education, the public high schools made great advances in the last quarter of the nineteenth century. In 1874, only twenty-one high schools met the standards of the state board of education, and only eight of them were in the northern half of the state; the rest were in southern Indiana towns, which speaks well for their concern. Churches were still responsible for part of that level of schooling, as the Catholics had opened nine high schools, the Quakers eight, the Methodists seven, the Presbyterians six, the Christian church four, with other denominations operating additional schools in smaller numbers. Two military academies were founded at Howe and Culver in the north. By the end of the century, Indiana had more than ten thousand schoolhouses and well over seven hundred high schools in operation. It was beginning to catch up with neighboring states. Consolidation has steadily reduced the number of buildings to fewer than a quarter of that peak figure. The general assembly began to support Indiana University in 1867 and took advantage of the Morrill Act of Congress and a private gift to establish Purdue University at West Lafayette, where it opened in 1874. Several more private colleges were founded in the northern part of the state.

Early in this century, the torch of learning was picked up in Gary, the state's newest city. William A. Wirt, a former student of John Dewey and school superintendent at Bluffton, boldly took new directions when he was appointed superintendent of the Gary schools in 1907. Wirt introduced the "platoon system," by denying students their individual permanent desks and giving them lockers, instead. While half the students were studying at desks in homerooms, the other half were in classrooms or activity rooms. Thus a given school building could accommodate almost twice as many students as formerly, an important consideration in a fast-growing city. By 1929, more than two hundred cities across the country had adopted the "Gary system."

Wirt broadened the curriculum to educate "the whole child." He believed in physical, artistic, intellectual, scientific, and manual training. Therefore his schools must provide, besides classrooms, laboratories, gymnasiums, pools, drawing and music studios, machine shops, printing shops, gardens, and an auditorium for student assemblies, plays, and debates. He sought specialized teachers for each subject. The school day was lengthened to eight hours, and he ran a summer school that attracted a third of the winter students. All these ideas are accepted today, but then the Gary system was visited by educators from all over the country. It was copied in New York City. Local residents appreciated it, too, after Wirt opened the school to adults in the evening. He enrolled as many of them at night as there were children enrolled in the daytime. Wirt remained in Gary until his death in 1938.

In the second quarter of this century, increased attention and support were given to the high schools, the two state teachers' colleges, and the two universities. Yet per capita expenditures for them remained very meager, compared to other states. Despite the depression of the 1930s, Governor Paul V. McNutt reminded the general assembly, "There are certain obligations which the state cannot deny even in periods of greatest stress: the care of its wards and the education of its children. In the one, the obligation runs to the unfortunate themselves. In the other, the obligation runs to society as a whole. The hope for future prosperity and leadership lies in trained men and women." [12]

Until well into the twentieth century, the state concentrated its support on the first eight grades of school. In 1900 only a small percentage of students who entered the first grade graduated from the twelfth grade. Even as late as 1922, only two-thirds of those who finished the eighth grade continued into public high school, and but little more than a quarter of them graduated. By 1950, one-half to three-fifths finished high school. In 1976 about 70 percent graduated. Indiana has come to have one of the highest literacy rates in the country.

Problems remain, of course. Local school boards often seem more interested in athletics than in academics. Indiana does not rank very high among the states in money appropriated for public schools, and it tends to be wary of federal aid. The dropout problem in high schools is diminishing but still serious. This is a national problem. Either there is not enough counseling, or the curriculum does not challenge marginal students, or the primary schooling was not mastered, or all of these.

In some towns, there were no blacks, and in the smaller cities the races were never segregated, but in other schools, where segregation did exist, integration began by court order in 1968. Generally, racial desegregation proceeded satisfactorily. However, there was trouble in Gary when children of white ethnic groups objected to blacks in their high schools. The chief problem area was Indianapolis, where Crispus Attucks High School was constructed for blacks in 1927 as a result of attitudes fos-

12. Indiana, General Assembly, House of Representatives, *Indiana House Journal* (1933), p. 103.

tered by the Ku Klux Klan. It is now 40 percent white, and the other high schools are mixed. No 100 percent white schools are left in the city, but a dozen all-black elementary schools remain. A plan to bus these students into suburban school districts was struck down in January 1977 by the U.S. Supreme Court. The teaching staff in Indianapolis is fully integrated.

Indiana University had never rated very high academically among the Big Ten universities of the upper Midwest. It seemed parochial in that, until after World War I, it was full of native students and native faculty. Gradually it achieved reputation and prestige under President Herman B Wells. As he had been a banker and dean of the School of Business Administration, without a Ph.D., he was thought by some of his faculty not to be a real scholar; but if that were true, he was something better: he was an able administrator who understood scholarship and encouraged research. He became president in 1937 and retired in 1962. In his regime, the university raised its standards steadily and improved its faculty, its press, and its academic rank. Its medical, dental, and music schools in particular and its library resources became highly regarded. Wells remained active as chancellor (fund-raiser and roving ambassador), a man much respected and widely admired.

Purdue University was long renowned for its schools of engineering, veterinary medicine, and agriculture. After World War II, it was ably directed by Dr. Frederick L. Hovde, who had been both a football star at the University of Minnesota and a Rhodes scholar at Oxford. After teaching at the University of Rochester and holding a key position with the federal Office of Scientific Research and Development, Hovde became president of Purdue University in 1946. He stayed until his retirement in 1971, because he liked the institution, and he put his stamp on it. Hovde broadened the engineering curriculum for "education of the whole man." He created a School of Humanities (with a department of philosophy), a Krannert Graduate School of Management for engineers who wanted to become business executives, and a School of Technology—a two-year program in practical engineering with an associate degree.

Purdue and Indiana University joined hands in establishing regional centers in Indianapolis and Fort Wayne, and each has its own branches elsewhere around the state with resident faculties. As a result, while the Bloomington campus of Indiana University showed an enrollment of 32,900 in the fall of 1976, 45,000 more students were enrolled at its seven centers, off the main campus. Similarly, Purdue counted 30,200 students in West Lafayette, and 12,700 more in the centers.

In 1965 the general assembly started giving money for state college scholarships, at least two for each county, and renewable for three more years. At the same time, the legislature created the Indiana Vocational and Technical College system, located in several cities. "Ivy Tech" is for high school graduates who are not seeking academic degrees, and it specializes in vocational training for particular jobs. It has enrolled 13,000 students in thirteen regions of the state.

By 1976 Indiana had caught up with its neighbors in the breadth and reputation of its public universities, although it was a relatively late arrival. The best of the private universities were Notre Dame and Butler; of the private colleges, probably DePauw, Earlham, Wabash, and Hanover. Total student enrollment in colleges made Indiana the fifteenth state in the country for numbers in 1975.

5

Hoosiers Move into
Cities and Factories

IN the post-Civil War decades, agriculture and industry in Indiana developed hand-in-hand. The number of farms increased steadily, from 132,000 in 1860 to a peak of 222,000 in 1900. Acreage increased as well, rising to 21,620,000 acres under cultivation in 1900. The chief crops that year were corn (although Indiana then ranked sixth in production among the states, and third in 1910); wheat (ranking, seventh); oats (ranking, tenth); hogs (ranking, fifth); and horses (ranking, eighth). The most prosperous farming counties were Benton, Carroll, Jasper, Tippecanoe, and White, all in the north, and Rush and Shelby in the south. County fairs reflected rural interest in prize-winning crops and animals, but in the long haul the livestock associations and the county agricultural agents were more effective than blue ribbons in educating farmers and stimulating higher production and better stock. Of course, profitable markets determined the diversity and emphasis of crops.

The primitive industries of the state grew out of her crops and timber resources: gristmills for grinding grain into flour and sawmills for cutting timber were found in several places in every county in 1860. Meat-packing plants were located along the Ohio and the Wabash for ready shipment of a perishable product. Beer was brewed and liquor distilled in several towns. Textile manufacturing included woolen and carding mills and two cotton factories. Engines for steamboats were built along the Ohio, along with some ships. Carriage and wagon works drew on the plentiful hardwoods, and furniture-making flourished in more than two hundred establishments. Shoes and leather were turned out in every county.

By 1900 the number of factories had more than tripled, and 156,000 persons were employed in 18,000 plants. Yet the leading four industries remained the same: milling, meat-packing, wood products, and distilling. Studebaker wagons of South Bend were nationally known. Foundries and machine shops made boilers as well as steam engines; blast furnaces using local and imported coal turned out railroad rails and castings. James Oliver's chilled-iron plows, made in South Bend, were achieving fame. Plate glass had been rolled at New Albany before the Civil War, but the discovery of natural gas in several eastern counties above the National Road in 1886 caused a boom in glass plants. They moved in from the East because of cheap fuel and temporary exemption from taxes. Such plants made tableware, windows, lamp chimneys, lantern globes, bottles, and fruit jars. Albany, Kokomo, Gas City, and Greentown turned out new patterns of tableware every year, along with kerosene lamps, bowls, jars, and all manner of novelties. Greentown was the home of the chocolate glass and golden-agate pieces so highly prized today by antique collectors. In Muncie, the Ball brothers from Buffalo began producing Mason jars for canning, and their name became a household identification. Indiana ranked eighth in the value of her manufactured products in 1900. Then the gas began to give out, and the glass plants in particular were abandoned.

Editors, retail merchants, politicians, and some farmers all welcomed industry and applauded its spread. The state government ventured to regulate the times of wage payments, hours worked per day, child and female labor, and safety devices. Craft unions were organized, and they were ruled legal in 1893.

Railroad mileage in the state tripled to 6,471 miles. Yet all of Indiana's industries were small.

After 1900 definite changes occurred in agriculture. The number of farms began to decline, falling to 166,600 in 1950 and 105,000 in 1976. Yet the number of acres under cultivation decreased less than 20 percent to 17,500,000 in 1969 and has stayed at that figure. In the 1970s, corn remained the largest crop, with Indiana still third in the nation. Soybeans are a new second crop, and Indiana ranks third in soybean production also. Wheat is the third-biggest crop, although the state stands ninth in production of it. Oats have fallen off considerably. Tomatoes waxed strong until 1945, when Indiana ranked next to California, and then decreased. In livestock, hogs still have top billing, related to corn production, and Indiana ranks third in the country. Production of poultry and eggs grew rapidly in this century, and Indiana stands seventh in output for poultry and eighth in eggs. Great hatcheries are found in Dubois, Jackson, and in Kosciusko counties; in the latter, the town of Mentone advertises itself as "The egg-basket of the Midwest."

When an English farmer and Oxford graduate came to Purdue University for a year of agricultural study in 1955, he was critical of some Hoosier practices: "There is," he noted, "the general air of untidiness, poor wire fences, gates of almost Anglesey dereliction. General 'extensiveness'—as if somebody had started to farm and had then gone away for a holiday." But down near Greentown he attended a cattle auction and saw a familiar gathering: "I was back in some East Anglican market. Same dull, glazed look when the cattle came in; same stolid powers of contemplation; and behind it were very shrewd, carefully professional minds weighing the job up to the last cent. I know that look." [1]

The sharp decrease in the number of farms and farmers after 1900 and the decline in agricultural acreage brought about

---

1. Nigel Harvey's comment, in *Travel Accounts of Indiana, 1679–1961*, edited by Shirley S. McCord (Indianapolis: Indiana Historical Bureau, 1970), pp. 282–283.

changes in the rural-urban balance of population. By 1900 two-thirds of the population was rural. With the rise of industry and the effect of World War I, Indiana remained in wonderful balance in 1920: fifty-fifty, urban and rural. Then the migration to larger towns and the growth of smaller ones began to tell. By 1950 Indiana was 60 percent urban, and by 1975 it was 67 percent urban and only 33 percent rural. Such subtle changes have affected its political stance, its educational outlook, and its social attitudes.

As industry increased in the twentieth century, Indiana never lost her agricultural base nor shed her celebration of small-town, rural-community virtues, to which citizens have clung with tenacity. Concommitant with this nostalgia for the simple life was the perpetuation of an attitude that lumped together those who were foreign-born or of some race other than Caucasian, cities, and big corporations as threatening to survival of small-town values.

Just before the turn of this century, a few Hoosiers became infatuated with "self-propelled vehicles," or the application of the internal-combustion engine to a carriage—in short, the gasoline automobile. Charles Black of Indianapolis built a car for himself in 1894 and drove it, but never went into that business. At Kokomo the same year, Elwood Haynes took drawings to the Apperson brothers' machine shop for a chassis on a buggy bed, mounting a one-cylinder engine attached to the wheels. There were problems, and changes were made before the test run, July 4, on the Pumpkinville Pike, southeast of the city. It worked! That was two years after Charles Duryea had demonstrated his car in Massachusetts, and one year after Henry Ford had built one in Michigan. Haynes and the Appersons incorporated to build more cars. They dissolved in 1902, and Haynes formed a company that made cars under his name, while the Appersons manufactured cars named for them. Meanwhile, other mechanics were turning out primitive cars: several in Auburn and South Bend and many in Indianapolis and Connersville. Of the 375 different makes manufactured in Indiana, only 16 lasted more than fifteen years. They were the American, Apperson, Auburn, Cole, Davis, Duesenberg, Elcar, Empire, Haynes, Lexington, Marmon, Maxwell, McFarlan, Studebaker, Stutz, and Waverley Electric.[2] By 1940 the auto industry in Indiana was chiefly in parts, rather than completed cars. The Indiana car builder that lasted longest, Studebaker, closed its South Bend factory in 1963. The big three of Michigan—Chrysler, Ford, and General Motors—all have branches in Indiana now.

As this résumé indicates, industry never became centralized in one city, like Illinois's Chicago or Michigan's Detroit. After the Civil War, Indianapolis was always much the largest city and became the center of a web of interurban lines, but it was surpassed industrially by the Calumet region and rivalled by Fort Wayne, South Bend, and Evansville. Smaller cities also had their growing factories.

If variety of manufacturing in Indianapolis characterized its industrial development, three disparate business leaders illustrated the wide range of economic philosophy found in the city. They bespeak experiences that have given Hoosiers unexpected maturity. David M. Parry (1852–1915) was very much the self-made man. Reared on a farm in Pennsylvania, he went into business in Rushville and in 1882 established a carriage works. Four years later he moved it to Indianapolis and built it into the largest buggy-and-carriage company in the world. He retired in 1911. He was also a railroad director, president of the Overland Automobile Company, and head of the Indianapolis Board of Trade. Parry was considered an able captain of industry who spoke up for big business, especially as president of the National Association of Manufacturers in 1902. He considered himself a "practical sociologist," but with a philosophy that was the antithesis of Robert Owen. Briefly, he was a foe of organized labor, arbitration, and government regulation. He thought Socialists were traitors, and he declared that "it is the

2. From "Indiana Autos: Indiana's Place in Auto History," by Wallace S. Huffman, *Indiana History Bulletin* 53, no. 3 (March 1976): 35–51.

business of every man to honestly get all he can.'' Like so many Hoosiers, he wrote a book, a satire on a future socialized state. He epitomized the autocratic and arrogant capitalist, yet aroused great fervor among employers who envied him. The 1930s exposed the flaws of his position and made him appear shallow and callous. His philosophy, shared by others, led inexorably to the industrial reform measures of the New Deal.

At the opposite end of the scale and coming along just after Parry's death was William Hapgood (1872–1961). In 1917 Hapgood inherited a small food-processing company in Indianapolis—Columbia Conserve—and decided to make it a laboratory of ''industrial democracy'' by inviting his employees to run it. He naively believed that anyone capable of working in the plant was capable of making management decisions, with a little coaching. The Columbia employees elected a committee to control production, sales, and wages, guided at first by Hapgood. Other Indianapolis manufacturers watched the experiment with varying incredulity or amusement. The committee promptly reduced hours, guaranteed an annual wage based on need, abolished time clocks, set up a pension plan, and shared in the profits so that they could as a trusteeship buy stock in the company. In the prospering 1920s, the company continued to roll along. By 1930 the employees owned a controlling interest. Hapgood wrote and lectured proudly about his ''experiment in industrial democracy.''

Then came the Depression, and sales declined; salesmen taken from the factory force quarreled about a new program. Hapgood's recommendations were vetoed, and the company would not reduce the number of employees. Wages had to be cut in half. A further complication was Hapgood's son, Powers, a Harvard graduate who had devoted himself to organizing labor unions. He found himself out of work in 1930 and came home to live with his father and involve himself in the Conserve company. On the side, he tried to unseat John L. Lewis from Lewis's position as president of the United Mine Workers, and he ran for governor on the Socialist ticket in 1932. With great forbearance, Hapgood allowed his son to organize a union in the company and introduce three radical cronies into positions of influence. Dissension and dissatisfaction followed. Early in 1933, when the employees' committee refused to act, the senior Hapgood fired the three radicals, and Powers Hapgood quit. Mr. Hapgood now found himself denounced as an autocrat, like any old capitalist, though he was trying to save the company from splitting into antagonistic factions. A long controversy ensued. To the amusement of Indianapolis, the Columbia Conserve Company was idled by strikers in 1942. Court action dissolved the co-operative plan, and the trustees' stock was distributed to the employees individually. It grew clear that the majority of workers wanted a management that would free them from responsibility for management and serve as an adversary in contract negotiations, someone on whom demands could be made and who would provide whatever benefits the labor contract granted. The company was sold early in 1953.

William Hapgood exhibited one of the same characteristics that hampered Robert Owen: so much faith in the common man that he was unable to learn from failure and readjust either his economic convictions or his view of human nature. Hapgood's son Powers, who mangled what he might have remedied, died in 1949.

But these two men, Parry and Hapgood, were not the only alternatives Indiana could offer. A third type of business executive started obscurely in 1876 in the heyday of patent medicines. Every drugstore was loaded with patent medicines, and their manufacturers' claims that the nostrums would alleviate or cure everything were widely advertised. Sales of patent medicines constituted a major part of a drugstore's income. The medical profession could do little to counter the situation, either with denunciations or prescriptions. Yet, quietly, in Indianapolis, a former druggist and Civil War veteran borrowed money to set about making his own attack by compounding drugs not for the public at all, but for physicians—drugs in which doctors might have enough confidence to prescribe. The druggist's name was Eli Lilly (1838–1898).

Lilly had learned pharmacy as an apprentice in Lafayette and had hardly opened his own shop before closing it to put on a uniform. Captain Lilly's Eighteenth Indiana light artillery was in several hot actions and distinguished itself at Chickamauga. He was promoted to colonel. In 1865 he was captured and held in a Confederate prison. After the war ended, Lilly decided to be a cotton planter in Mississippi, but a crop failure and the death of his wife drove him back north with his small son. He opened a drugstore in Paris, Illinois, and remarried, but found that being a retailer interested him less than compounding his wares. He was hardly a conspicuous success when he moved to Indianapolis and started his new venture, at age thirty-eight. And how naive to challenge the established patent-medicine business!

It was a lonely, uncertain struggle for a long time. Eventually, the federal government took a hand in regulating drug products after passage of the Pure Food and Drug law of 1906, and public health education began to make consumers more critical. Today, the preponderance of patent medicines has been greatly reduced. On its hundredth anniversary, in 1976, the Eli Lilly Company stood serenely at the top of the "ethical drug" profession, as it is called, having earned the respect of the medical and pharmaceutical practitioners. Colonel Lilly had found a way that few perceived was possible to combat an evil. As for economic and sociological theories, the company struck no pose, but simply treated its employees as human beings ("The first responsibility of our supervisors is to build men, then medicines") [3] and jealously guarded its reputation for the purity and efficacy of its products. Because of the company's early practice of providing paid vacations, pensions, and other fringe benefits, employees had no interest in unions. During the Depression, no one was thrown out of work. Privately owned until 1952, the company steadily poured money into research, a policy that the publicly owned corporation continues. From that investment has come Iletin (insulin), Merthiolate (antiseptic), Darvon (pain-

3. E. J. Kahn, Jr., *All in a Century, the First 100 Years of Eli Lilly and Company* (Indianapolis: Eli Lilly Co., 1976), p. 41, quoting Eli Lilly.

killer), Duracillin (penicillin), Keflin (antibiotic), and Treflan (weed-killer).

In World War I, the Eli Lilly Company equipped a base hospital in France; during World War II, it manufactured blood plasma for the American Red Cross at cost, a steadily decreasing figure as techniques were improved. The company also provided two hundred medicines for the armed forces. The business grew steadily under Colonel Eli's son and his two grandsons and became a model for socially responsible private enterprise. As an extra dividend, the Lilly family created a foundation, now fourth-largest in the country, which grants millions of dollars annually for good works.

Indiana's second great industrial area is the Calumet, the northwest sector of Indiana, named for a sluggish river that flows east to west, then turns north and empties into Lake Michigan. The word is Indian and refers to a tobacco pipe; the shape of the river suggested the word to early French travelers.

In 1905 the Calumet held about 19,000 inhabitants—12,000 in Hammond, the rest in East Chicago and in Whiting, where oil refineries flourished early. Gary did not then exist. At that time, the United States Steel Company decided it could produce and sell more steel if it built the most modern mill somewhere in the Midwest. The factor governing location was access to Great Lakes shipping, in order that the mill might receive iron ore from northern Michigan and Minnesota. The corporation selected a site at the south end of Lake Michigan and bought up nine thousand acres of land and slough, a narrow strip between the Calumet River and the lake, extending for seven miles along the shore. It then formed the Indiana Steel Company in 1906 to build and operate the mills. This company in turn formed the Gary Land Company to lay out a town for the steel workers. The land company and the town were named for Judge Elbert Gary, chairman of the board of U.S. Steel.

Wider streets than usual at that time were staked off. The land company expected the main street to run east and west, so that all employees would live within a short distance of their work. The principal north-south street, where many residents eventually preferred to settle, was called Broadway and extended as far south as the Wabash Railroad tracks. Liquor was to be sold in only two places, which the company thought it could control. Otherwise, the company did not intend to build houses or stores or regulate the lives of the inhabitants. After laying off lots, it protected purchasers from speculators by requiring that houses be built within eighteen months after purchase, and the water, electricity, and gas would be supplied from facilities constructed to supply the steel mills. Black dirt was brought in to cover the sand so that grass would grow. A huge harbor had to be constructed for lake ships at a cost of $2.5 million.

All kinds of people flocked in, American and foreign-born, black and white, many single or without their families. Bunk houses and tents were visible first, resulting in a huge boarding-house business. Vice flourished, along with drunkenness, fighting, and thievery. Early Gary was not unlike earlier western towns.

The town was immediately incorporated in 1906. Tom Knotts was made president of the town board of trustees and later elected mayor. He was a former schoolteacher, insurance agent, and policeman in Hammond. A man of strong convictions, who thrived on opposition, he sought a new career in Gary by devoting himself to fighting the Indiana Steel Company until he was defeated at the polls in 1913. Knotts paved Broadway and extended it southward beyond the Wabash tracks, but neglected the east-west streets. A streetcar franchise was given to his friends in opposition to a group proposed by the company. It was Knotts who hired William A. Wirt—mentioned earlier—to start a new public school system. Knotts's chief adversary was William P. Gleason. Gleason, who supervised construction of the mills and remained the iron-handed superintendent of operations until 1935, was very generous toward the development of the city. He was instrumental in having the Gary Land Company build a brick school in 1908 and rent it to the school board until the board could buy it. The company likewise gave the site for a city hall, and four frame buildings for a Catholic hospital. It created two big parks and presented them to the city after Knotts left office; gave land for a new Carnegie library, for a Methodist church (Gleason was a member), for a new hospital, and for an armory. Judge Gary himself gave $200,000 for a YMCA in 1910, and the company furnished it. The Indiana Steel Company started pensions for its employees in 1910 and hired a visiting nurse for their families.

Unlike other Indiana towns, Gary thus received a considerable boost from its corporate founders. Steel production began in 1908, after arrival of the first iron ore in the harbor and with the lighting of the first blast furnace. The Indiana Steel Company was called the greatest steel plant in the world, and much of the heavy work was done by machines. Gary hoped to become Pittsburgh's rival. By 1910, the town had nearly 17,000 inhabitants. Half were foreign-born; 383 were blacks. Two-thirds were males, and 4,200 of them were employed in the mills. A bridge company and a tin-plate works were added as subsidiaries of the Indiana Steel Company.

World War I, with its demand for steel, boomed the city. Three thousand Negroes were there by 1916, recruited as workers from Chicago, southern Indiana, and the Deep South. By 1920 the population exceeded 55,000. Meanwhile, Gary had suffered its first strike, which was watched closely by the rest of the state.

If the Indiana Steel Company was paternal in looking after the welfare of its workers, it was autocratic in setting hours and wages. Steel-making is a peculiar business, in that blast furnaces must be kept in continuous operation. If allowed to go out, they must be torn down and rebuilt, a costly repair that takes several months. They can be banked, an operation that interrupts work for only a few days. As a consequence of that fact, the furnace tenders worked in two shifts of twelve hours each, seven days a week—or an eighty-four-hour week without a day of rest. Fifteen percent of the work force was on such shifts. The others worked twelve hours a day for six days a week, or seventy-two hours. These hours did not seem bad to foreigners, who endured as much or more in their native countries, and the pay was good. The American Federation of Labor, however, was promoting an eight-hour day, and the company discharged any employee who joined a union. Judge Gary could not see any need for unions. What the company overlooked was not simply the long, exhausting hours, but the corruption of foremen, who threatened the men under them with being fired, in order to extract favors from the work force.

In 1917, after the United States entered the war, the War Labor Board prohibited the firing of employees for joining unions. The AFL appointed a committee to organize the iron and steel workers. William Z. Foster was its secretary, and he came to the Calumet region in September 1918. On October 1, the Indiana Steel Company inaugurated an eight-hour day, but hired no more men. Employees continued to work twelve-hour shifts but received time-and-a-half pay for the last four hours of each day. Of the two newspapers in Gary, one was antiunion and the other criticized the company. U.S. Steel insisted that the union organizers were Bolsheviks, or Communists, and, ultimately, that was true enough of Foster.

When the War Labor Board expired in 1919, strikes began. Samuel Gompers, president of the AFL, and Foster were both rebuffed on requesting a meeting with Judge Gary. The several union presidents in the Chicago district voted to strike on September 22, in spite of Gompers's warning that they would fail. Gary was the storm center.[4]

No one knows how many steel workers stayed away from the mills after September 22. Some workers lived in the mills, where they were supplied by the company, which could always reach the mills by ship. Some furnaces were banked, but a week later the mills were still operating at 50 percent of capacity. The Negroes, who had not been unionized by the AFL, kept on working, and so did most of the native white Americans. Primarily the foreign-born struck, although they were under the

4. Lowell A. Moore, *The Calumet Region, Indiana's Last Frontier* (Indianapolis: Indiana Historical Bureau, 1959).

false impression that the union would continue paying them. The company brought in Negro strikebreakers and also Mexicans, who had come to the region during the war as railroad workers.

After the strikers attacked a streetcar full of workers on October 4 and dozens were injured, the mayor asked for state militia. Two days later, the strikers defied the mayor's ban on parades and marched and jeered the watching militia. Governor James P. Goodrich called for federal troops from Fort Sheridan, Illinois. A thousand came, and their colonel established martial law in the city. Soldiers patroled the streets. The strike was over, but Foster didn't know it.

By November 26, all the mills were back to operating at 90 percent of capacity. The colonel arrested troublemakers and put them to work cleaning the streets. Russian haranguers were turned over to the immigration service for deportation. In general, the foreign-born respected military force, out of old fears, and went back to the mills. On January 8, 1920, the last pickets were withdrawn and the troops pulled out. No shot had been fired. Foster went on to join the Communist party and became its candidate for president in 1924, 1928, and 1932.

Largely because of its foreign-born element, Gary did not take prohibition seriously. In 1922, federal agents swooped down on 127 bootleggers and uncovered a few stills of wholesale capacity. More stills were seized there than in any other Indiana city. In January 1923 a grand jury indicted 62 persons for violation of the liquor law, including the mayor, county prosecutor, sheriff, city judge, president of the city's board of public works, three policemen, and three prominent lawyers. All but the sheriff were convicted. But after the mayor was released from the penitentiary in 1925, he was re-elected on the Republican ticket in 1929! Small wonder that the rest of Indiana looked upon the Calumet as atypical, an exotic region somehow not part of the state.

Outside of Gary, Indiana could supply in modest amounts some of the first World War's demand for trucks, tanks, airplanes, ships, ammunition, oil, uniforms, food, and medicines.

The needs of the Allies were felt late in 1914, and demand increased over the next two years, before the United States became involved. Like the rest of the country, Indiana prospered from the war in Europe, although German and Irish elements in the state's population objected at first to taking the side of Great Britain and France. More and more workers left farms for factories, and northern cities drew southerners. The number of wage-earners in manufacturing, mining, transportation, construction, and government grew by 50 percent between 1910 and 1920.

Another effect of World War I was that old industries based on utilization of soil and timber were overshadowed by those based on iron. In the change, crafts began to disappear; the manufacturing process was broken down into small steps that could be performed by unskilled workers and the whole put together on the moving assembly line. That kind of production not only resulted in boredom and loss of pride in the finished item, but forecast the decline of craft unions. The American Federation of Labor, composed of crafts, was torn apart by the emergence of the Congress of Industrial Organization, which sponsored unions of predominantly unskilled laborers representing all the employees of a given type of industry, like the separately organized miners—such as steel workers, rubber workers, auto workers, or electrical workers.

Indiana industry was hit hard by the Depression. As the demand for coal and limestone collapsed, due to the decrease in manufacturing all over the country, half the population in the south was left without means of support. Factory production in the north declined, and employees were thrown out of work. Only Lilly and Ball kept their men on the payroll. Interurban lines into Indianapolis began to fail. A state Department of Public Welfare was created in 1936 to administer relief grants, and federal projects kept some of the unemployed at work. Unions found membership as they never had before, but strikes helped little. Some banks closed, others reopened by assessing their stockholders, and a few came through unscathed, without calling on their stockholders or causing their depositors to lose a dollar.

Gary was particularly depressed. It had a population of 100,000 when the steel mills began to cut back on employment. In 1931 they were running at 24 percent of capacity, and the next year that figure dropped to 15 percent. Most of the 3,500 Mexicans there had never become citizens, and hundreds of them began to go home. The American Legion in East Chicago raised money for their repatriation and secured a special rate from the railroads. They helped send back to Mexico 1,800 from East Chicago and 1,500 from Gary in 1932. Even so, Lake County went bankrupt from its relief load, and the Reconstruction Finance Corporation lent it $750,000 in 1933 to provide jobs on public works and for food orders. By the time that money was used up, the federal government had assumed much of the relief burden. Company unions were dissolved in 1937 after a pact with the CIO was signed.

World War II had greater impact on Indiana than did the first war. One aspect was the development of training facilities. Camp Atterbury, an enormous complex 8 by 12½ miles in size, was carved principally out of Bartholomew County for training whole divisions. It added Wakeman Hospital for the war wounded, and a stockade for 12,000 prisoners of war. Bunker Hill Air Station, below Peru, trained naval flyers, and Baer Field near Fort Wayne tested army bombers. Jefferson Proving Ground above Madison tested ammunition and parachutes. Crane Ammunition Depot covered 62,700 acres in Martin County, to store and issue all types of shells for the navy. The federal government also bought up 250 farms in La Porte County to serve as location for an ammunition-loading plant.

The other aspect was the conversion of industries to war-matériel production. General Electric of Fort Wayne, International Harvester of Fort Wayne and Indianapolis, and Studebaker and Bendix Aviation of South Bend became military contractors. Servel Refrigerators of Evansville turned out wings for fighter planes, cartridge cases, and land mines. Shipbuilders on the Ohio worked for the navy. Allison and Curtis-Wright of Indianapolis made aircraft engines and propellors. Rex Manufacturing Company of Connersville made depth bombs for the navy, mortar shells, and rockets. Eli Lilly and Company of Indianapolis produced blood plasma at cost, as well as other medicines. And soon, the need for steel and oil focused on the Calumet region. At the start of the war, three hundred factories in the state held defense orders. The number of wage earners almost doubled between 1940 and 1950.

After the war, the surge of industrial growth continued for a few years. New plants were attracted to the state by moderate taxes, transportation facilities, available energy, reasonable unions, and lack of a state debt. The main trends in manufacturing have been increased use of assembly lines and interchangeable parts, mechanization of the process as far as possible, supplanting of steam as a source of energy by electricity and oil, and, in consequence of all that, an increased productivity per worker. Inevitably these developments have increased the amount of regulation by state and federal government. Locally owned small industries have been taken over by national corporations, and their plants have expanded into other cities. The prefabricated-home business of Lafayette boomed, and the construction of mobile homes in numerous small factories dots the Elkhart area.

Again, Gary was vitally affected. The 1960 census showed its population to be 178,000; it soared above 180,000 by the middle of the decade, but in 1970 it shrank to 175,000, of which less than 47 percent were white. In 1967 Gary elected a black mayor, Richard Hatcher, attorney and former councilman, even though he received no aid from the county Democratic organization. Hatcher set out to smother the graft, corruption, and vice that had flourished in the city. He obtained federal monies for new housing and increased the inspection of substandard dwellings. He started a training program for unskilled workers and reduced air pollution. He reorganized municipal government to make it more efficient and responsive. By encouraging black participation in government, without handing patronage jobs to incompetents, he gave blacks a new concern for the city and ruffled many of the old guard. He supported busing for school integration. Not surprisingly, he was re-elected in 1971 and again in 1975.[5]

Mayor Hatcher could not stop the flight of whites from the city. Small communities to the south and east in Lake County jumped in population. The Burns Harbor development east of Gary attracted more industry. Gary suffered accordingly, as have other depleted cities. Crime has increased. Business places have closed, partly because of the opening of South Lake Mall, ten miles away. Several stores in 1976 stood vacant or were boarded up; others had iron grates over their windows. A thirteen-story Holiday Inn downtown opened only its first seven floors in 1971 and then closed altogether in 1975. Few whites were seen on the main streets.

The *Post-Tribune* reported in the summer of 1976 that the population of Gary was 161,000. The other three cities of the Calumet also lost population. Never a typical Hoosier city, Gary has become even more exceptional, and the whole region has seemed different; not much agriculture, the large percentage of foreign-born, the rougher politics, the orientation around Chicago—all caused it to be written off by the rest of Indiana as a region apart, with its own culture.

After a lull in expansion, a resurgence of the state's industrial growth occurred in the late 1960s and lasted until the recession of 1974. In the same period, 60,000 young men were drawn from the work force into the Vietnam conflict. In 1976 the largest employer in Indiana was General Motors, with more than 50,000 employees in nine plants in six cities. Second was United States Steel, with about 23,000 workers, down from 30,000. Then came Radio Corporation of America, International Harvester, General Electric, and Eli Lilly. Per capita personal income in Indiana, however, was not up to the national average.

Some odd businesses survived, however. Buggies and wagons

5. Alex Poinsett, *Black Power Gary Style: The Making of Mayor Richard Gordon Hatcher* (Chicago: Johnson Publishing Co., 1970).

were still made in Huntingburg until 1952. The St. Clair Glass works at Elwood turns out paperweights. Musicians declare that the finest bassoons manufactured in this country are made by Fox in South Whitley. Coffins by Hillenbrand are big business in Batesville. Nappanee is noted for kitchen cabinets by Mutschler and Coppes. Clabber Girl baking powder is still a Hulman product at Terre Haute. Down in Grantsburg, Frank Fancher still makes superior ax handles by hand. Indiana is second among the states in growing popcorn, and Orville Redenbacher of Valparaiso sells a gourmet variety. Cracker Jack is made in Middlebury. So all is not lost to bigness and homogeneity.

In most states, industrial development was accompanied by a rise in foreign immigrants. That was not true in Indiana for a long time. In the period from 1860 to 1880, Indiana was less affected by European newcomers than almost any other northern state. In 1860, the state counted 9 percent foreign-born, the highest ratio it ever attained. In a population of almost 2,000,000 in 1880, ranking the state sixth in size in the whole country, the foreign-born numbered only 144,200, or 7.3 percent; whereas Michigan had 388,500 for 24 percent of its population, Ohio had 395,000 for 14 percent, Wisconsin had 405,500 for 44 percent, and Illinois had 583,500 for 23 percent. Indiana hardly counted at all in that league. It was more homogenous in population than its neighbors above the Ohio River.

Of those foreign-born in 1880, 55 percent were Germans, 17 percent were Irish, and most of the remaining 28 percent were British, French, Swiss, and Scandinavians—all north European. Most of them were not difficult for Indiana's white Protestants to assimilate, though most of the Irish and many of the Germans were Roman Catholics. The flow of immigration to the United States rose over the next several decades to flood tide and altered several eastern cities and states. Yet in Indiana the increase was barely noticeable, from 144,200 in 1880 to 151,300 in 1920. What that meant, of course, was an almost steady decline in the ratio of foreign-born: 5.6 percent in 1900 and 5.2 percent in 1920. The latter figure was so low that Indiana had the highest proportion of native-born white population of any state in the Union.

The only significant change in those forty years was in the mix. Southern and eastern Europeans appeared on the scene. As many of them were unskilled workers, they gravitated toward the industries of the Calumet, where they amounted to a quarter or half of the population of the cities of the extreme northwest for a time. Nevertheless, by 1950 the foreign-born were only 2½ percent of the whole state population. In 1970 that small percentage had dropped further to 1.6 percent. The 83,000 then counted were more than half made up of 11,000 Germans, 13,000 from the United Kingdom and Canada, 6,400 from Asia, 5,900 from Poland, 5,100 from Yugoslavia, and 5,000 from Mexico.

When restrictions against Negro immigration were dropped after the Civil War, a good many blacks entered the state. Still, by 1880, Negroes constituted only 2 percent of the total population. By 1920 they made up 2.8 percent of the whole. Indianapolis absorbed much of the new Negro migration, including those moving up from the state's Ohio River cities. The black population of Indianapolis reached 11 percent in 1920, while the percentage in Jeffersonville and Evansville declined sharply. Many Negroes were attracted to the industries stimulated by World War I. In rural areas, blacks were seldom seen; in 1920 two counties reported none, and nineteen more counties had less than ten each.

Yet Indiana remained attractive to Negroes, and their numbers increased here. In the 1970 census, they numbered over 356,000, which was more than in Kentucky, but less than in Ohio, Michigan, or Illinois. They then amounted to 7 percent of Indiana's population, while the national average was 11 percent. They constituted 11 percent of the state's urban dwellers and .6 percent of the rural. There has been a Negro press in Indianapolis since 1879. An influential class of black merchants and professional people and political office holders has developed.

The prejudice of older white Hoosiers against the Negro dissolved into disinterest; they were conservative, even in their re-action to forced integration. Just as there was no particular ob-jection to the expansion of Negro housing in Indianapolis, there were no riots in conjunction with integration of the schools. Outside of the Calumet, no ethnic groups existed to band against the blacks, and there was no Chicano wedge to compete with less-skilled blacks for jobs.

It would be a grave mistake to assume that, because Indiana has become industrialized (ninth-largest manufacturing state in the country), agriculture is no longer important. A state that in 1976 ranked third in corn, hogs, and soybeans, seventh in poul-try, and eighth in eggs is still a major farming state. Indiana stands eighth in agricultural products. Cash receipts from farm-ing exceed the value added to raw materials of any state in-dustry—steel, machinery, or auto parts. Moreover, one-third of its people are considered rural, and more than that percentage are reluctant urban dwellers. Probably more than half the state's population cherishes farm memories and folkways. This nos-talgia shows itself in one way through the persistence of county fairs (every county has one, and five have two fairs!) and the popularity of the state fair in Indianapolis. In 1976 the state fair attracted 1,194,000 visitors—a new record—during its eleven-day run. Grossing more than $3 million, it is reputedly the only state fair in the nation that pays all its costs. Obviously, Hoosiers enjoy themselves at fairs.

Another effect of nostalgia shows itself in the conservation movement. State and federal forests cover more than 320,000 acres. Another 59,000 acres are formed into state parks and rec-reational areas well scattered. Five of the state parks contain inns, an innovation of the 1930s attractive to many families. Be-sides good food and comfortable rooms, the parks provide na-ture trails, swimming pools, tennis courts, evening lectures, a toboggan run in the north, and a reconstructed pioneer village in the south. Fish and game preserves add another 75,200 acres for sportsmen. Wyandotte Cave in Harrison County is the third-largest cave in the country. Hoosiers have gone far toward pre-serving the wilderness and open spaces. This development owed much to the vision and energy of Richard Lieber, head of the Conservation Department from 1919 to 1933. Born and educated in Germany, Lieber came to this country in 1891 and settled in Indianapolis. He was made chairman of the State Park Commission in 1915 and, until his death in 1944, never lost interest in conservation.

Indiana has not appeared to be enthusiastic about industrialization. As long as manufacturing could be small, locally distributed, and family-owned, it was warmly embraced for providing jobs. But when, in the third and fourth decades of this century, it grew into corporate factories, impersonally managed and unionized and sensitive to outside economic currents, the older Hoosiers were pricked by doubts and questions. No alternative seemed viable, so they went along with what the age called progress, yet remained nostalgic for the older, simpler life. They were not unlike the Indians they had dispossessed, finding some aspects of the new industrial culture attractive (cars, movies, household appliances, medicines, television sets), but also upsetting to traditions, family rituals, seasonal rhythms, closeness to the soil, and the old pace of life. It forced a choice of values, and Hoosiers were less sure of themselves. They shook their heads about Gary. They applied the brakes to rapid change and the senseless search for novelty. Venturesome outside entrepreneurs found them reluctant actors on today's stage.

6

Any Number Can Play:
Hoosiers in Politics

T is said that the first words of a Hoosier baby are: "I'm not a candidate for office, but if nominated I will run, and if elected I will serve." The false modesty fools no one. Most Hoosiers enjoy their politics. They participate more intensively than citizens of many other states. And such intensity is not without its excesses.

In certain neighboring states, by contrast, candidates for elective offices and aspirants for political appointments are often viewed with suspicion. They are considered, by and large, to be a little lazy, incapable of holding a good job in the world of business, and possibly dishonest or at least of elastic moral scruples. Not always, in Indiana; politics there is mainly a respectable profession, although recognized as having its own rules. The political arena attracts occasional able candidates, although not so many professional people or successful business executives as are needed.

Those who defend and take pride in Indiana's excessive interest in politics assume it was a Hoosier characteristic from the beginning of settlement. It was not. Actually it had an inauspicious start about 1809, after a dormant gestation period of twenty-five years after the first pioneers arrived. Before that time, early settlers showed a surprising lack of interest in government or in voting. Such indifference was not unusual; it was common throughout the trans-Appalachian West after the Revolutionary War.

The social revolution ignited by the War for Independence was slow in spreading. The founding fathers developed an elaborate theory of government resting on the consent of the governed. The "sovereignty of the people" had a nice ring to it, but how was that consent to be elicited and that sovereignty expressed? The Revolutionary generation had a philosophy, rather than a program. The mechanics of election seemed simple. At the outset, candidates for office were selected by a few educated and wealthy gentlemen meeting around a dinner table or on a veranda. The deferential majority of people of lesser social standing, used to leaving government to their "betters," accepted those candidates and voted orally as they were told. The next step was a caucus of elected officers at state level or at congressional level, who nominated their friends for various offices. There was no campaigning: a man "stood" for office at the behest of his friends; he did not "run" for it.

Meanwhile, independence and abundant new land to settle were stimulating the growth of a sense of equality, and the leadership of the elite was questioned. That was a repetition of what had happened along the tidewater in the seventeenth century. It grew from pride in accomplishment and self-respect. These traits became especially strong on the western frontier, where few of the elite ventured, and where the pioneers were cut off from contact with the federal government and, at most, had only one nonvoting delegate in Congress. There was a sense of proprietorship in "our land" that was transferred locally to "our government." By 1800 there were two distinct political parties: the Federalists, who gave way to the National Republicans; and the Democratic Republicans, who soon dropped the second word. The former were followers of the ruling families of Virginia, New York, and Massachusetts; they believed in a strong central government that would encourage commerce and industry. They knew what was best for the country and how to provide it. The National Republicans faded out in 1832, and a new party of Whigs included them and some old Jeffersonian followers. The second major party moved from the leadership of Jefferson to that of Jackson, advocating a limitation on the powers of the central government, less government in general, more offices elective and for shorter terms, and broader suffrage. Yet the Democratic Jefferson did not hesitate to veto bills passed by Congress, the representatives of the people.

With the establishment of opposing political parties, adherents were eagerly sought. How could they be attracted? They must be allowed to choose candidates and define issues. A convention of each party was called to make nominations. Then to get out the vote was a formidable task among a scattered people who thought of the national government as remote and rather mysterious. It is surprising today to learn how few people bothered to vote at first.

Candidates were persuaded to run and people to vote by two exercises: the government was whittled down so that the electorate could understand its operation and the issues; and the combined executive, legislative, and judicial duties of the Northwest Territory were separated into three functions as soon as possible. Within them, particular jobs and terms of office were defined. Thus the qualifications for office tended to be so reduced that a good many men felt they could discharge the prescribed duties. Candidates then proliferated. As time went on, more offices were made elective, and as a check on responsiveness, terms were shortened.

The second step was the inauguration of campaigning for office. The end in view was to arouse the electorate to vote. Candidates announced their positions, friends spoke or wrote on their behalf, newspapers endorsed or opposed them, pamphlets and broadsides appeared. Candidates for president in 1836 made appearances and spoke a few times. By 1840 resort was made to slogans and symbols, parades, public meetings, endorsements, costumes, song books, free drinks, endless speeches, even sermons—all covered by violently partisan newspapers, with all the ballyhoo so taken for granted today. The campaign featured such slogans and symbols as "Tippecanoe and Tyler, too," log cabins and hard cider, "Van, Van, the used-up man," ad nauseum. If dignity was sacrificed and demagoguery invited, these were the risks of popular appeal. To have no preference or no opinion became synonymous with ignorance or shameful neglect.[1] Americans gradually came to believe in the political process and to relish making government a servant. Hoosiers have been remarkably American in retaining that enthusiasm.

We see the political process beginning to operate in Indiana Territory first in 1809, when Jonathan Jennings announced his own candidacy for delegate to Congress. He made it clear that he was a man of the people, opposed to Thomas Randolph, a Virginia aristocrat, a proslavery man, and the favorite of Governor Harrison. Jennings won, but the total number of votes cast was only 911, probably about 23 percent of the eligible voters in the territory.

By 1816, when forty-three delegates met to write a state constitution, the Democrats were in the majority, and Jennings was made president of the convention. Foes of slavery were also in the majority. In 1824 just under 36 percent of the eligible voters in Indiana voted, and the state went Democratic, while the country elected a National Republican president. Perhaps that discrepancy aroused Hoosier males, because four years later they turned out in force—66 percent of those eligible—to help put Democrat and westerner Andrew Jackson in the White House. When Jackson ran again in 1832, almost 70 percent of the eligible Hoosiers voted, and the majority favored him. Then the rip-roaring campaign of 1840 pitted Democratic President Martin Van Buren against a Whig candidate, William Henry Harrison, whom Hoosiers of short memory now revered, and led to the remarkable turnout of almost 83 percent of the voters!

1. I am indebted to conversations with Professor Shaw Livermore of the University of Michigan History Department for this view of evolving participation in government after the Revolution.

Because Harrison lived in Ohio, the turnout of voters there was a little higher, but Michigan and Kentucky showed substantially fewer.

Indiana's constitution of 1816 contained no provision for amendment. Instead, it called for a referendum every twelve years to consider whether a convention to revise, amend, or change the constitution should be called. The question was put and voted down in 1828 and 1840, but in 1846 a special vote authorized by the legislature favored a constitutional convention, and a second in 1849 confirmed it. The demonstrated interest in voting and the rising sense of equality sparked a desire to increase the number of elective state offices, to limit local and special legislation, to protect the state from financial extravagance, and to encourage primary schools. At the same time, annual sessions of the general assembly were considered too frequent and too costly, not conducive to less government. Governor James Whitcomb also favored biennial sessions, because they "would afford a better opportunity to the people of knowing what the laws are, before they are modified or repealed." [2] Revising state constitutions was in fashion: Illinois and Wisconsin were changing theirs, and Ohio was talking of it.

Indiana's 150 delegates were authorized to be chosen in 1850. Two-thirds of them were Democrats; 74 were born in the South, and 70, including the 13 native to Indiana, were born in the North. About half had served in the legislature; 42 percent were farmers, and 25 percent were lawyers.

The convention met in Indianapolis on October 7, 1850, and sat until February 10, 1851. If Indiana's first constitution was brief and Jeffersonian in philosophy, the second was long and Jacksonian. County government was recognized and allowed to exercise some of the duties hitherto thrown on the state legislature. Pushed on to the courts was the business of granting divorces, allowing name changes, and granting exceptions to revenue laws. The new charter flatly prohibited the state from going into debt. Robert Dale Owen of New Harmony argued

2. *Indiana Statesman,* October 13, 1850.

that "one generation of men have no moral right to contract a public debt so vast that the next generation, and perhaps that which follows it, shall be loaded down with taxes, to discharge the interest and repay the capital." [3] Most Hoosiers still felt that way, 125 years later.

Besides the governor and lieutenant governor, the offices of secretary of state, treasurer, auditor, and judges were made elective. The governor could not succeed himself, but must wait out a term of four years. The charter required common schools but said nothing about colleges or even high schools. An elected state superintendent supervised the common schools. An amendment process was spelled out.

The convention added two remarkable provisions, one wise and one disgraceful. The first limited biennial sessions of the legislature to sixty-one days. By and large, that limitation has been prudent: some foolish bills have been lost in the crowded docket of a session's last few days; the appropriation bill has been passed well before the current fiscal year ends; the state has enjoyed twenty-two out of twenty-four months free from legislative meddling; and the consensus has been verified that representatives and senators can make up their minds in two months as well as they can in six or eight or more. Not until 1971 was a change made to allow annual sessions again of the general assembly, yet still limited in length.

The despicable provision of 1851 was not simply that free Negroes and mulattoes could not vote, but that they could no longer come into or settle in the state. To the outsider, it might appear that Indiana was flooded with blacks and wished to shut off the flow; but that was not true. In 1850 the state contained only 11,300 people of color, who made up about 1 percent of the population. The prohibition reflected attitudes of racial prejudice, bigotry, and hatred. White Hoosiers of that era regarded Negroes as inferior, likely to become public charges or crimi-

3. *Report of the Debates and Proceedings of the Convention for Revision of the Constitution of the State of Indiana, 1850* (Indianapolis: A. H. Brown, Printer to the Convention, 1850–1851), p. 658.

nals, undesirable to educate, impossible to associate with, and therefore uncomfortable to have around. Their humanity extended only to the point of not wanting to enslave black human beings or torture them physically and of wishing to help them by deporting them to Africa. White Hoosiers were consistent only in not wanting Negroes imported to provide cheap labor. With what seems an obvious sense of guilt, that extraordinary article was submitted to the voters separately from the constitution itself, but it was approved by a vote close to that by which the constitution was adopted. In 1864 the U.S. Supreme Court, doubtless affected by the war, declared the article contrary to the U.S. Constitution, but the words were not removed until 1881.

Nationally, the Whig party was going offstage. In the debate over the extension of slavery, the Liberty and Free-Soil parties rose in opposition. Then a Native American, or Know-Nothing, party, which was anti-Catholic and antiforeign, appeared in the 1850s and spread through Indiana. Those three elements—old Whigs, Free-Soilers, and Know-Nothings—fused and carried the state elections that year. They called themselves the People's party, but sent delegates to the new Republican party in 1856. Four of their members came to prominence. Schuyler Colfax of South Bend went to Congress, became speaker of the House, and served as vice-president under President Ulysses S. Grant. Henry S. Lane presided at the state convention and became U.S. senator. Oliver P. Morton, a disgruntled Democrat from Centerville, became governor and U.S. senator. George Julian, an abolitionist from Centerville and vice-presidential candidate on the Free-Soil ticket in 1852, had served in Congress and was destined to reappear there in 1860 and remain for a dozen years. Fellow townsmen, Morton and Julian despised each other.

The new political party showed strength in 1856 only in the northern half of the state. The southern counties remained Democratic and helped elect Ashbel P. Willard of Floyd County governor and James Buchanan president. The Irish in Indiana were considered to be a solid Democratic bloc, some of them accused of selling their votes. The Germans, it was felt, were dividing, some of them turning to the new party. Results were different elsewhere in the Old Northwest: Republicans carried Michigan, Ohio, and Wisconsin, while Illinois divided between Buchanan for president and Republicans for state offices. Kentucky, like Indiana, stayed Democratic. The Republican label was adopted in Indiana in 1858, and although the party turned its back on the Know-Nothings, it would not adopt as strong an antislavery position as Julian wanted. It narrowly won control of the state legislature that year. Women's rights were being advanced then, but were too easily ridiculed by men. Besides, in Indiana, rights for women were considered to be contrary to Scripture.

A deal was made in the 1860 election. The new Republican party smelled victory and was solidly for candidate Abraham Lincoln. Since the party did not want to renominate the once-defeated Oliver Morton, it turned to Henry Lane. The latter preferred to be U.S. senator and was counting on a Republican legislature to send him to Washington. Consequently, Morton was glad to run for lieutenant governor and thus advance to the vacated governorship. Julian ran for Congress. Everything turned out as planned. Almost 86 percent of the eligible voters in Indiana went to the polls, exceeding the national average by 5 percent.

During Reconstruction, most Indiana congressmen supported the Radical Republicans and defied the more moderate presidents Johnson and Grant. Interest in voting continued to rise. In 1868 almost 92 percent of the eligible voters cast their ballots, possibly because Schuyler Colfax was running with Grant and still fighting those "murderous traitors," the Southern Democrats. In 1876, when it appeared that the Democrats might win the presidency after sixteen years, Hoosiers turned out 95 percent strong, far above the national average of 81.8 percent, which is the highest ever recorded for the country. Indiana's participation exceeded that of all its neighbors and has led modern political scientists to wonder if perhaps some Hoosiers voted twice.

Since that date of a century ago, the national voting average has declined steadily to 53 percent in 1948, and, after a little recovery, fell back to 53 percent in 1976. Indiana's participation declined and then rebounded: in 1948 it was 67 percent, but in 1976, 75 percent. That seems to be proof that interest in politics in Indiana runs stronger than in neighboring states and in the country as a whole. It is not easily explained, beyond the fact that it has become traditional.

Since politics attracts lawyers, it is instructive to know how easy it was in Indiana to become a lawyer. The constitution of 1851 contained a provision that "Every person of good moral character, being a voter, shall be entitled to admission to practice law in all courts of justice." [4] Thus one became a lawyer simply by announcing that identity or profession and hanging out a shingle. That remarkable section was not stricken out of the constitution until 1932. Since lawyers were articulate and practiced effective public speaking, they frequently turned to politics and campaigned vigorously. Hoosiers loved campaign oratory. "Come, give us a speech," was an invitation to entertain, regardless of substance.

Another reason for the intensity of politics was the evenness of party strength after 1876. Indiana became a "swing state," eagerly courted by the two major parties. A deflection of 1 or 2 percent of the voters would determine which party got the electoral votes. Hence every vote counted, and the party organization was devoted to getting out the voters and combatting indifference. Within the state, each party was promised federal appointments and frequently given national nominations. Victory within the state meant patronage to dispense, of course, for the spoils system was not only approved but felt to be necessary.

Dissatisfied midwestern farmers after the Civil War formed a social and educational organization called the Patrons of Husbandry. A local chapter was known as a grange, and this word replaced the more formal title. The first chapter in Indiana was

4. Indiana, *Constitution* (1851).

organized in Vigo County late in 1869. At the beginning of 1875, there were almost 3,000 granges in the state, with a total membership of close to 60,000 men and women. They promoted marketing of crops and co-operative buying of seeds, fertilizer, and implements. They also campaigned for lower freight rates. The Grangers entered politics by fostering the Independent party and elected 13 members of the Indiana General Assembly in 1874. The next year delegates from twelve states formed the National Greenback party, with two Hoosiers as chairman and secretary. The Greenback party was not the last third party to be born in Indiana.

In the election of 1876, the state went Democratic—for Samuel J. Tilden as president, former Governor Thomas A. Hendricks of Shelbyville as vice-president, "Blue Jeans" Williams (a loyal Granger) as governor, and a majority in the general assembly. Although long a rural state, Indiana had never before elected a farmer to the governorship. For the presidency, however, Tilden fell short of victory by one vote in the electoral college, and the electoral commission decided the dispute in favor of Republican Rutherford B. Hayes of Ohio. Nevertheless, the Democrats were restored to a party of strength in Indiana.

Each party had a strong man regarded as boss, whose approval was needed by aspiring candidates for office. Oliver P. Morton was perhaps Indiana's first political boss, running state politics from 1860 till his death in 1877. A Democratic legislature chose a Democrat to succeed him in the Senate—a former congressman from Terre Haute and an orator called the "tall sycamore of the Wabash": Daniel Voorhees. Voorhees remained in the Senate until 1896, but wielded little power in the Indiana Democracy, as Thomas Hendricks seemed to be in control and ultimately achieved the vice-presidency under Grover Cleveland.

The election of 1888 stained Indiana's honor, coming as it did soon after the trial and imprisonment of two election officials for forging tally sheets in 1886. The chairman of the Republican National Committee, Hoosier William Dudley, supposedly advised county chairmen in the state that money would be available to corral and bribe "floaters" to vote Republican. The party carried the state, but even the victorious governor considered that the ballot had been polluted. Payment to floaters, who were willing to sell their votes, tinged all elections in the latter part of the nineteenth century. Some floaters were shifted around, so as to vote twice. That kind of fraud was usually treated as one of the ways the game of politics was played. A partial remedy was adoption of the Australian secret-ballot system. It did not eliminate the need to monitor the counting of ballots, where corruption might rise again.

In the campaign of 1896, Albert J. Beveridge, James E. Watson, and Tom Taggart appeared prominently on the state scene. An Indianapolis attorney, Beveridge supported McKinley for president, was elected to the U.S. Senate in 1899, and became an ardent imperialist during the Spanish-American War. After re-election in 1905, Beveridge was defeated in 1911 by having become a devoted follower of Teddy Roosevelt. He ran for governor in 1912 along with Roosevelt's bid for the presidency as a Bull Moose or Progressive party candidate. Both men lost. Beveridge was a popular orator, but had grown impossibly conceited and had become a political maverick. He turned to writing and produced a creditable *Life of John Marshall* in four volumes. It won the Pulitzer Prize in 1920. His subsequent biography of Abraham Lincoln had little claim to scholarship.

James E. Watson practiced law in Rushville and was elected to Congress in 1894 as a Republican. He was defeated for governor in 1908, but was elected to the U.S. Senate in 1916 to fill out a term and was re-elected in 1920 and 1926. Watson became part of the conservative wing, working for high tariffs, banks, railroads, and corporations, and opposing the League of Nations and free immigration. As an isolationist, he favored a big navy. Yet he supported woman suffrage and steered the constitutional amendment through the Senate. Watson was ambitious enough to oppose Hoover's nomination in 1928, hoping to secure it for himself. His weakness was that he never rose above party politics and was in his element presiding over seven state Republican conventions. Yet during his period of prime influence, two Democratic governors were elected. After he was defeated for the Senate in 1932 by Democrat Frederick Van Nuys, he remained in Washington to practice law.

Tom Taggart, born in Ireland, was a little older than either Beveridge or Watson. He became Democratic auditor of Marion County, mayor of Indianapolis from 1895 to 1901, and chairman of the state Democratic committee. Yet while he was boss and supposed to carry his party to victory at the polls, six of Indiana's eight governors were Republicans. From 1900 to 1912, Taggart was on the Democratic National Committee, and he was a delegate to all the national conventions from 1900 to 1924. Appointed to the U.S. Senate for a few months, he lost the special election to Watson. His other interests kept him an affable figure in state politics; he owned and managed the French Lick Hotel, where politicians often gathered, and he was chairman of the Fletcher National Bank.

Taggart's rival was Will H. Hays, a lawyer in Sullivan who loved the political arena and attracted many friends. Hays became state chairman of the Republican party in 1914 and moved on to become national chairman in 1918. President Harding rewarded him with the familiar post of postmaster general, where, to everyone's surprise, Hays raised morale and efficiency, armed employees to reduce mail robberies, and effected great savings. Then in 1922 he went to Hollywood, where his talent for getting quarrelsome people to work together was exercised as president of the Motion Picture Producers and Distributors of America. His suavity and high moral standards were badly needed in Indiana just then; he might have resisted the Ku Klux Klan.

The Klan story is a dark chapter in Indiana politics, a stain on Hoosier intelligence, an aberration that should not be forgotten, even though it cannot be fully explained. It was in part the delayed price paid for Indiana's long indifference to public education, for suspicion of people who were "different," and for a numbing insularity. On this fertile ground the seeds of bigotry were sown by an effective appellant to prejudice and a gifted

confidence man—one D. C. Stephenson of Texas and Okla-
homa, who migrated to Evansville in 1920. Stephenson was
then twenty-nine, a rather good-looking, heavyset blond who
had served as an officer in World War I. He organized the veterans in Evansville and managed to run for Congress as an anti-
Prohibition Democrat. Soundly beaten, he became a Dry Republican.

At that time, the continuance of the Russian Revolution
stirred a "red scare" in the United States, abetted by a frightened attorney general. It created an atmosphere of suspicion
about foreigners or any groups exhibiting nonconformity or critical of government policy. Renewed patriotism was called for to
"save" the country from Bolsheviks. The Ku Klux Klan advertised that it stood for "Americanism," family life, the church,
and Prohibition, in addition to native white supremacy. The
Klan had been revived in the South, and the Klan Imperial
Wizard, a Dallas dentist, appointed Stephenson an organizer for
several midwestern states. He was most successful in Indiana,
with his amiable, persuasive manner, his dramatization of im-
pending dangers, and his indifference to truth. He played on a
latent intolerance in certain Hoosier minds. It was a profitable
business, too, and Stephenson loved luxury. He kept four dollars of each initiation fee of ten dollars, and, so rumor held, a
similar cut from the sale of robes and masks. He appointed
organizers throughout the state, and the tendency of Indianans
to be joiners was exploited. How many Hoosiers became Klansmen is not known; the invisible Klan itself spoke of 250,000 to
500,000 at its peak, an obvious exaggeration; more reliable estimates suggest a total of 100,000 to possibly 200,000. Whatever the figure, Stephenson grew rich in a hurry. He moved to
Indianapolis and in 1923 was appointed Grand Dragon of Indiana. Had he settled in another state, would he have achieved
the same brief success he enjoyed in Indiana? It is an intriguing
speculation.

His white-robed followers frightened some Catholics, Jews,
Negroes, and foreigners by burning crosses as warnings, parad-
ing silently through city streets, and reviving the old Horse

Thief Detection Association to flog deviants, raid moonshine stills, and threaten burnings of buildings for protection money. Then they would ostentatiously interrupt Protestant church services to leave large "offerings" of money. A few newspapers ridiculed them, but only an occasional clergyman spoke against them.

What Stephenson wanted most was power and place. He hoped to become a U.S. senator, if he could gather political strength. In the May 1924 primary election, the Klan supported Republican Secretary of State Ed Jackson (who had granted their charter for organization) for governor, and Jackson won the nomination. In local elections, Klan-backed candidates usually won. The Imperial Wizard then fired Stephenson for alleged involvement with a girl and appointed another "Grand Dragon." Stephenson had been twice married, but operated in Indianapolis alone. He called a Klan mass meeting, denounced the wizard, and separated the Indiana organization from the national Klan. In the fall election, Jackson won the governorship, which was remarkable, since Governor Warren McCray, also a Republican, had been forced to resign earlier in the year and go to prison for using the mails to defraud in attempting to get himself out of debt.

At the inaugural ball, January 12, 1925, Stephenson was the most sought-after guest. There he met an Indianapolis girl of twenty-nine whom he began to date, while legislators beat a path to his suite of offices. He began to brag that he was the law in Indiana. At this pinnacle of power, his gross appetites betrayed him. In March he forced the young woman to accompany him on a night train to Chicago, during which ride he assaulted her severely, being something of a sexual sadist. Frightened then, he and two henchmen took her off the train at Hammond to a hotel. Bitter and despondent, she procured poison and took it. Stephenson finally drove her back to Indianapolis and callously put her in his garage. Later he had her taken home, where she died—but not before she had dictated a long affidavit to her attorney, Asa Smith, and her physician, Dr. John Kingsbury. With great courage, they had Stephenson arrested and aided the prosecution. Suddenly all the virtues claimed by the Klan wilted. Stephenson was found guilty of second-degree murder for withholding medical treatment from a dying person and was sentenced to life imprisonment. In 1951 he was paroled, only to violate the conditions (it was lechery, again), and be returned to prison. Pardoned in 1955, he disappeared, a complete nonentity.

In Stephenson's fall, the Klan edifice collapsed. The *Indianapolis Times,* which had announced its opposition to the Klan in October 1924, now went after the municipal remnants of the corrupt organization and was awarded a Pulitzer Prize in 1928 for its campaign. The Indianapolis mayor was found guilty of the Corrupt-Practices Act and jailed. Six council members were indicted for taking bribes; they resigned and were fined. A Muncie judge was impeached. The former Republican state chairman was imprisoned on a conspiracy charge. Governor Jackson was indicted for bribery but was saved by the statute of limitations. Klansmen ran for cover. The nightmare was over. Mayor Reginald Sullivan, a Democrat, restored honesty and dignity to Indianapolis government.

There has been no recovery of the Klan. Could there be? Newsmen say no. They cite the higher level of general education today, the number of blacks in public office, and the exposure possibilities of television. There was still a Grand Dragon in Indiana in 1976, but he has bolted the national Klan and tries to keep alive a minuscule independent state organization. It falters from indifference. Perhaps the vast majority of Hoosiers now not only disagree with Klan objectives but also despise its alarming juvenility—in costume, secrecy, and ritual. The madness of the early twenties suggests that if Hoosiers examine warily any new and radical appeal for change, they are less cautious about embracing conservative and reactionary movements. The latter seem safer, because they can be modified and liberalized as experience indicates, whereas a radical step releases forces that seldom can be contained again.

When William D. Pelley, on the run from North Carolina, moved to Noblesville in 1940 and founded the Nazi-like Silver

Shirts and a new religion called Soulcraft, Hoosiers showed little interest. He was arrested in 1942, found guilty of sedition, and sentenced to prison.

In the aftermath of Klan revulsion, new leaders emerged in the Democratic party. Taggart was finished; he was succeeded by a much shrewder power broker who was rising in Logansport. Frank McHale, another Irish Democrat, had gone to the University of Michigan, where he won All-American honors as a football tackle. He graduated from the university's Law School in 1916. After serving in the air force in World War I, he organized the Cass County Post of the American Legion. He was building a law practice in 1924 when the Ku Klux Klan paraded through Logansport on the Saturday before Labor Day. To his disgust, he saw the local American Legion band participating. The robed knights were carrying a big American flag flat, so that money could be tossed onto it. This misuse of the flag as a receptacle did not irritate McHale so much as the repeated and proprietary orders by marching Klansmen for the bystanders to remove their hats. When McHale refused, the parade stopped. Confronted, he stepped off the curb and defied anyone to knock his hat off. Looking at him, the Klansmen saw a man six feet tall, immensely broad in the shoulders, and weighing 230 pounds. After some grumbling, the parade moved on, leaving at the curb a partisan dedicated to defeating every bigot connected with that white-sheeted tribe. The Klan paper reported the incident afterward and said that the stranger held a gun in each hand when challenged.[5]

McHale was elected state commander of the American Legion in 1926 and was followed in that office by Paul V. McNutt, dean of the Indiana University Law School and a graduate of Harvard Law School in the same year that McHale finished at Michigan. McHale tried his organizing skill by managing McNutt's election to the post of national commander of the American Legion in 1928. National headquarters had been established

5. This incident was told by McHale to Irving Leibowitz and published in the latter's *My Indiana* (Englewood Cliffs, N.J.: Prentice-Hall, 1964), p. 121.

in Indianapolis. McHale attended the Democratic National Convention that year, the first of eleven to which he was sent. The two men moved into state politics, McHale managing NcNutt's victorious campaign for the governorship in 1932. McHale transferred his law practice to Indianapolis and set about writing progressive legislation for McNutt: the state income tax, the alcoholic beverages act, the utilities tax bill, and the revised public service commission act.

McNutt was the strongest governor since Morton. He reorganized a rather creaking state government of 169 departments, bureaus, and agencies into eight functional departments. That change and the imposition through the legislature of a state income tax led to cries of dictatorship. Organized labor, however, supported McNutt until a general strike in Terre Haute in 1935 led him to send in state troops. McNutt instituted a "2 percent club"—that is, all state employees were expected to contribute 2 percent of their salaries to the party's coffers. It was such a good idea that the Republicans copied it, but in more recent years it was rarely enforced. Still, it was brash politics, not expected from an academic dean.

Despite Depression needs, McNutt left office with a ten-million-dollar surplus for his Democratic successor. Seemingly, he could win any office, and he had the highest ambition. Also, like Morton, he was arrogant. After he took the oath of office, he let it be known to his cohorts that he should be addressed as "Governor." That is a pretentiousness Hoosiers will not accept. If you're known as "Al" in your home town, it doesn't matter if you're elected president; you're still "Al" to your old friends. It's what you are as a private person that counts (a frontier tradition), not your offices, titles, degrees, honors, or fortune. Whatever you have accomplished or acquired is attributed to luck, and you're no different fundamentally from your poor, uneducated, or unrecognized neighbors. That is a fiction, of course, but it is preserved by the graciousness of those who have moved ahead. Perhaps it makes an easier society. Thus industrialist Homer Capehart sponsored a Republican "cornfield conference" at his farm in 1938 and won a following that put him in the U.S. Senate six years later. In 1940 Indiana's Wendell Willkie, his forelock dropping down on his forehead, clinging uncomfortably to his podium, apologizing for his lack of oratorical ability, talked "common sense" to his "neighbors" across an invisible back fence—and routed the established politicos.

President Franklin Roosevelt recognized McNutt's success, his intelligence, his attractive appearance, and packed him off to the Philippines in 1937 as High Commissioner, rather than allow him to gain a national following as a cabinet secretary. Nevertheless, McNutt returned in 1939 to direct the Federal Security Administration. McHale, who had gone on to the Democratic National Committee and influenced federal appointments in the state, started a campaign to win McNutt the presidential nomination in 1940, never guessing that Roosevelt would seek an unprecedented third term. A disappointed McNutt, who could not even salvage the vice-presidential nomination, had to watch his old campus rival at Indiana University, Wendell Willkie, sweep the Republican nomination without previous political experience. Later McNutt headed the War Manpower Commission, returned to the Philippines as our first ambassador there, and died in New York in 1955. If he was the right man for the presidency, he became available at the wrong time. McHale outlived him by far, dying in January 1975, full of honors, widely respected for his integrity and acumen, and well liked for his geniality, public services, and private generosity.[6]

While the major parties were fighting each other as usual, Indiana brought forth a more exceptional political figure than anyone the two older parties produced. Yet, aside from a city clerkship and one term in the state legislature, Eugene V. Debs of Terre Haute never was elected to public office. Born in 1855, he quit high school to become a railroad worker and advanced only as far as locomotive fireman before he jumped the track to be unpaid secretary of his local Brotherhood of Locomotive Fire-

6. *Indianapolis Star,* January 27, 1975.

men, while clerking at Hulman's wholesale grocery. In 1880 he was elected national secretary-treasurer of the BLF and editor of its magazine. His concern for the unskilled railroad workers and the separation of the four skilled brotherhoods (firemen, engineers, conductors, and brakemen) led him to organize an industry-wide American Railway Union in 1893. Despite objections from the brotherhoods and from Samuel Gompers, president of the American Federation of Labor, the new union pulled in a big membership, limited to whites, and Debs was made president. It was a personal achievement, for the men trusted him, and that trust grew into affection and devotion.

When the Pullman Company of Pullman, Illinois, reduced their employees from 5,500 to 3,300 in 1894, as the result of depression, and slashed the wages of those remaining on the payroll while maintaining the level of its rents in company housing, Pullman employees joined the ARU and called a strike. George Pullman refused to arbitrate or even to talk to the union. Debs's union then decided not to handle the Pullman cars on any railroad. The strike was not popular with the other railroad unions, and the railroad bosses obtained a court injunction against the ARU leaders. Debs ignored it. President Cleveland (for whom Debs had campaigned) sent troops to Chicago, despite objections from the governor. Debs was arrested for contempt, and the strike ended after two months' duration.

Sentenced to six months in jail. Debs emerged as a convinced Socialist. It has been reported that he studied Socialism while in jail, but his biographer doubts that he read much of anything. Rather he was visited by two Socialists who assured him that their philosophy of government and economics would alleviate all the miseries of laborers that so aroused Debs's sympathies. Debs was a profound sentimentalist, a temperament that explains also his close friendship with another Hoosier sentimentalist, James Whitcomb Riley. It is doubtful whether Debs had any understanding of economics, currency, banking (he distrusted all banks and refused to use them), free markets, profits, risks—in short, of capitalism. And one wonders how much he comprehended Socialism and its political ramifications.

What he saw about him were powerful corporations with political influence managed by ruthless executives devoted to profits and hostile to unions. In Socialism he saw a promised realization of the Utopianism described in Edward Bellamy's popular novel, *Looking Backward,* a book he found tremendously appealing. He believed that Socialism's glib slogan of "collective ownership of the means of production and distribution" was a panacea for the common laborer's distress, and he devoted the rest of his life to pursuit of that goal. He was gentle, sincere, stubborn, forgiving, extremely generous, sympathetic to anyone in need, and a man people liked and revered. Intellectually, he was naive and sometimes inconsistent; yet, he was a forceful speaker.

In 1897 he transformed the emaciated ARU into the Social Democratic party and later fused it with the Socialist Labor party. Meeting in convention at Indianapolis in 1900, the delegates nominated Debs for president. He polled less than 100,000 votes nationally, and soon the uneasy alliance of several factions broke up in quarrels. At another Indianapolis convention, a new organization was formed and called simply the Socialist party. Debs was its candidate for president in 1904, 1908, 1912, and 1920. His best showing was in 1912, when he garnered 37,000 votes in Indiana, and more than 900,000 nationally.

As a pacifist in World War I, he was imprisoned for attacking the Wilson administration, until pardoned by President Harding late in 1921. Debs returned to a great civic welcome in Terre Haute; the people loved him, although they thought his political philosophy was invalid. When he died in 1926, ten thousand attended his funeral. He was, as political journalist Edward H. Ziegner said, a remarkable man, but he was hardly, as John B. Martin called him, "the most important figure Indiana has produced." [7] Norman Thomas, the next quadrennial Socialist candidate for president, never approached Debs's appeal in Indiana.

---

7. Edward H. Ziegner, "Indiana in National Politics," in *Indiana, a Self-Appraisal,* edited by Donald F. Carmony (Bloomington: Indiana University Press, 1966), p. 48.

Third parties have never prospered in Indiana. Hoosiers would rather be winners than defeated idealists. They want to put their votes where they will count. Norman Thomas received only 21,400 votes in 1932 in the depth of the Depression. Henry Wallace got only 9,650 as Progressive candidate in 1948. George Wallace registered 243,000 votes in 1964; the citizens of foreign extraction in Lake County preferred him. In the 1976 election, all three minority candidates together got a total of only 21,700 votes, less than 1 percent of the total cast.

In the latter part of the nineteenth century, Indiana was zealously pursued by both political parties, and it held to that role into the twentieth. In the 1912 election, besides offering a presidential candidate in Debs, Indiana had former Governor Tom Marshall of Columbia City running for vice-president on the victorious Democratic ticket with Woodrow Wilson. Four years later, Marshall was renominated, and former Senator Charles Fairbanks of Indianapolis was the Republican vice-presidential candidate with Charles Evans Hughes. Either way the election went, Indiana was spotlighted. After that, however, the Republicans began to regard Indiana as a safe state, bound in thralldom to the party. With the exception of 1932 and 1936, when the state favored Roosevelt, that was true. But something happened in 1940: the state went Republican nationally because of native son Willkie, but it continued to favor a Democratic governor and elected Henry Schricker of Knox. Schricker was a reticent, shrewd campaigner, with all the homespun Hoosier virtues, a man one instinctively trusted. After being out of office one term, as required, he was re-elected in 1948—the first governor ever to achieve such a comeback—while the state again favored Republican Tom Dewey. Clearly, Indiana was separating itself from national politics.

At the county level, politics was much the same rough game. Elmer Davis of Aurora, radio commentator and director of the Office of War Information, tells of the 1938 election in Indiana as it affected Senator Frederick Van Nuys's bid for re-election on the Democratic ticket. The party had nominated him reluctantly, because Roosevelt wanted to purge him for having opposed Roosevelt's scheme to enlarge the Supreme Court. The campaign came just after the Munich crisis, during which Hitler grabbed Czecho-Slovakia and gave a piece of it to Poland. At state Democratic headquarters, a heavy vote was expected from Lake County, but instead Van Nuys received only a light majority. What happened was that the Democratic leaders were Poles, but many of the voters were Czechs, who now despised the Poles and voted Republican. Gloom settled over party headquarters until word came in that the vote count from Vigo County would be delayed. It was delayed, indeed, for eleven days, and when the returns came in, "by happy coincidence, they were just enough to put Fred Van Nuys over." [8]

Recently, the Democrats have brought on stage some attractive new faces with more flexible goals than Republicans offered. In 1958 liberal Mayor Vance Hartke of Evansville succeeded the reactionary Senator William Jenner of Bedford, defender of Senator Joseph MacCarthy and defamer of General George C. Marshall. Matthew Welsh of Vincennes, another Democrat of intellectual achievement, was elected governor in 1960. Welsh's general assembly added a state sales tax to an increased income tax. Birch Bayh of Terre Haute beat the redoubtable Senator Homer Capehart in 1962. Both senators were re-elected twice, but Hartke fell in 1976 to a younger Republican, Richard Lugar, a Rhodes scholar and former mayor of Indianapolis. (Indiana has another Rhodes Scholar in Congressman John Brademas of South Bend.) Welsh was followed by another Democratic governor, Roger D. Branigan, Lafayette attorney and Hoosier wit. Branigan's Democratic legislature repealed a "right-to-work" law (prohibiting closed-shop contracts that required workers to join a union) that a Republican assembly had enacted in 1957. Reapportionment of the legislative districts in 1966 gave urban counties more representatives and ended the old rural domination of the general assembly, a long-delayed reform.

8. Elmer Davis, *Old Indiana and the New World* (Washington, D.C.: Library of Congress, 1951), p. 9.

At the other end of the political spectrum, the John Birch Society was organized in Indianapolis at the end of 1958 by Robert Welch, a visitor from Massachusetts. National headquarters is in Massachusetts, but the former dean of the University of Notre Dame Law School served on the society's council, and two staff organizers set up a dozen or so American Opinion libraries in the state and a speakers' bureau. It appealed only to the most hidebound of conservatives, and its endorsement became a liability.

Republicans recaptured the statehouse in 1968 and in 1972, also giving majorities to Richard Nixon in both elections. Unusual progressive legislation followed. Under Governor Edgar Whitcomb, a new schedule of annual assembly meetings was enacted: in an odd-numbered year, the assembly may meet for sixty-one sessions, but not beyond April 30; and in an even-numbered year, a shorter meeting of thirty-one sessions is permitted, but not beyond March 15. Further, Indianapolis was allowed to extend its boundaries to coincide with Marion County, the result being a single government for city and county and a much larger metropolitan population to report. In 1976, for the first time, the governor was allowed to succeed himself, and Governor Otis Bowen of Bremen (pronounced *Bree-man*), projecting an image of the fatherly family physician, won a second term. More of a moderate than a conservative, Dr. Bowen carried the state for President Ford. Bowen's first administration established commissions to study mass transportation, solid waste disposal, malpractice insurance, pollution and flood control, and the regular reassessment of real property. The state property tax was reduced, the sales tax was doubled, local units of government were allowed to impose an income tax, and collective bargaining authority was granted to certain government employees (including teachers), but strikes were outlawed.

In all that ferment, the day of the powerful state political boss in Indiana seemed to be over. Parties have lost their steadfast adherents. A reliable survey in 1975 found only 23 percent of Indiana voters acknowledging that they were Republicans. Probably a slightly larger percentage would label themselves Democrats. What that means is that about half the voters are Independents, the bugaboo of all political bosses. To be sure, the Independents are not organized; they have no platform; they are either indifferent or hostile to the old parties, but will vote with one or the other. Still, no state chairman can count on delivering a majority for his slate of candidates, just as it has been demonstrated that no union leader can deliver the votes of his union. With a few minor exceptions, people no longer vote in blocs. Hoosiers can discriminate and they will split their votes.

Further, in 1975 the legislature deprived party conventions of the right to nominate candidates for governor, lieutenant governor, and U.S. senator, and decreed that such nominations must come from a direct-primary vote. That was a blow to "horse-trading" among party leaders. They can nominate lesser officers only—and even that they now do by secret ballot. So when the county or district chairman calls on the delegates to "vote for Joe," he can't discipline those who don't, because he can't identify them.

Another factor reducing bossism is the diminishing amount of patronage available. Not as many of the faithful can be promised appointments, in the Jacksonian tradition. The civil service or merit system makes more sense to the taxpayers. The state of Indiana now has about 25,000 employees. Only 8,000 or so have jobs that are filled by patronage (3,000 in the highway department). Their contributions to the party treasury are resisted by their unions, and a new act of Congress in 1976 outlawed the old 2 percent club. Party loyalty must be freely given.

Candidates must now win votes from Independents, and by their own exertions, as well as carry their own party membership. Extremists can't do it, as candidates from Debs to Wallace have demonstrated. Success at the polls requires not only some charisma, but attention to issues. That is good. But the decay of party discipline enlarges the role of lobbyists, who focus on a single issue and support the candidate that lines up their side of the question, regardless of what other positions he assumes. That is not good.

Hoosiers have taken their post-Revolutionary political heritage and expanded it into wide participation without the most scrupulous standards. They have never lost their enthusiasm for the game of governing themselves; they have not grown cynical or indifferent. Though Hoosiers show greater interest in politics than do citizens of most states, candidates of the highest talents are still scarce.

7

Hoosiers as Authors and Artists

*T*HE fine arts in Indiana number two: writing and painting. They have overshadowed every other art, and they have attracted innumerable practitioners. Authors and artists have been producing in Indiana for generations. If geniuses have not emerged, a lot of people have expressed themselves and engaged large audiences, more than in almost any other state.

When that perennial Chautauqua lecturer the late Opie Read first appeared in Fort Wayne, he announced that he was aware of Indiana's literary reputation and therefore, if there was an author in the audience, would he please stand. Whereupon the audience rose, en masse. Mr. Read recovered himself in time to notice one old man still seated and called attention to him as one Hoosier who was *not* an author.

"Oh, no, he writes too," someone said. "He's just deef and didn't hear the question."

The story was told by George Ade and others with such variations that it may be a piece of folklore. Indiana's literary productivity is one of those phenomena that is easily exaggerated. Investigation, however, has revealed some startling statistics. Books have indeed been a major product in this state. The number of people who write is all out of proportion to the population.

The first attempt at a bibliography of Indiana authors, with

155

biographical sketches, was made by R. E. Banta of Wabash College in 1949.[1] Even after eliminating writers of genealogies, textbooks, lab manuals, and law books, and those who had contributed only to magazines and newspapers, and limiting consideration to those authors who published before 1917 (the first hundred years of statehood), Mr. Banta came up with 950 eligible writers—an average of almost ten new book authors a year for a hundred consecutive years. Moreover, almost no one was a one-book author—all that in a state whose population had grown to about 2,800,000 in 1916.

After that initial research, the Wabash College librarian, Donald E. Thompson, added a sequel that carried the investigation ahead for fifty years to 1966. He wound up with 2,751 more Indiana authors, a few of them belonging in the 1816–1916 volume.[2] Even if those who might be claimed with equal justice by other states were omitted, there would remain a grand total of at least 3,600 authors! Yet it is not simply that so many Hoosiers wrote that gave the state its reputation; it is, rather, the indisputable fact that some of them produced one best-seller after another and so compelled attention to Indiana. The long-time librarian of Purdue University, John Moriarty, examined the authorship of the ten best-selling novels each year from 1900 to 1940. By allowing ten points for the number-one best-seller, nine points for the second best, and so on, down to one point for the tenth book on the list, he totaled up a score of 213 points for Indiana authors in that long period. That score was exceeded only slightly by New York's 218 points—from a population four times larger! The next-ranking states hardly offered competition: Pennsylvania, 125 points; Virginia, 102; and Kentucky, 94.

Studying an extended list of best-selling fiction from 1895 to 1965, Mr. Thompson found that the distance between New

1. R. E. Banta, *Indiana Authors and Their Books, 1816–1916* (Crawfordsville, Ind.: Wabash College, 1949).
2. Donald E. Thompson, *Indiana Authors and Their Books, 1916–1966* (Crawfordsville, Ind.: Wabash College, 1974).

York and Indiana authors widened: 460 points for New York versus 288 points for Indiana, with Pennsylvania again third. So Indiana remained in second place, despite the disparity in population with New York and Pennsylvania. If readers find these comparisons difficult to credit, here are the names of some particular authors claimed by Indiana:

Humorists George Ade, Don Herold, Kin Hubbard, and Emily Kimbrough; mystery writer Rex Stout, creator of Nero Wolfe; historians Charles and Mary Beard, Claude Bowers, Glenn Tucker, and Richard O'Connor, and O'Connor is a biographer, as well; juvenile authors Martha Finley, of "Elsie Dinsmore" fame; Mabel Leigh Hunt; Annie Fellows Johnston, of the "Little Colonel" series; Miriam Mason, Elizabeth McElresh, Jeannette Covert Nolan, Augusta Stevenson, and Ann Weil; historical romancers Lloyd C. Douglas, George Barr McCutcheon (who invented a whole country—Graustark), Charles Major, Maurice Thompson, and Lew (*Ben Hur*) Wallace; poets Robert Underwood Johnson, James Whitcomb Riley, and William Vaughn Moody; social commentators and critics Elmer Davis, director of the Office of War Information; Janet Flanner, the *New Yorker*'s Citizen Genet; George Jean Nathan; war correspondent Ernie Pyle; and novelists Theodore Dreiser, Edward and George Eggleston, Margaret Weymouth Jackson (also known for her short stories), Meredith Nicholson, David Graham Phillips (who wrote twenty-three novels in ten years), Gene Stratton Porter of "the Limberlost," Booth Tarkington (who twice won the Pulitzer Prize), Kurt Vonnegut, Jessamyn West, William E. Wilson, and Marguerite Young.

Writing started early in Indiana. The first author is shared with Kentucky: Jesse Lynch Holman was born there, but he migrated to Indiana in 1811, when he was twenty-seven, and spent the rest of his life here. The year before he came, he had published a novel, *The Prisoners of Niagara,* and later in life he wrote much poetry for Indiana newspapers. From that date, the race began. Production increased slowly in the 1830s and 1840s, with poets now largely forgotten, essayists writing on religious questions, scientific articles from New Harmony, and first-person confessions of criminals and alcoholics. An anonymous novel about Indiana was published in the state in 1845, along with a few other examples of fiction. Meredith Nicholson believed that Mrs. Julia Dumont of Vevay, the teacher of the Eggleston boys, was the first to attract Eastern attention, with her *Life Sketches from Common Paths: A Series of American Tales,* published in New York in 1856. These stories had already appeared in western periodicals; indeed, Mrs. Dumont's first story was printed in 1824.

There was a lull in writing during the 1860s, doubtless occasioned by the war. Then in 1871 appeared Edward Eggleston's *The Hoosier Schoolmaster.* He was followed by Lew Wallace and Riley, and the literary boom was almost an explosion. If there was a Golden Decade, it was the period from 1900 to 1910. At that time Riley, Major, Thompson, Tarkington, Ade, Nicholson, Moody, Phillips, McCutcheon, and Mrs. Porter were turning out one best-seller after another. The furious pace was maintained for another two decades, which was remarkable endurance.

The fact that an unusually large number of people born and educated or long resident in Indiana have turned to writing, and that a respectable percentage have achieved great popularity, has to be accepted as truth. But why did they? The answer can only be speculation, based on a few relevant facts, such as the geography of the state, the people it attracted, the character and institutions it developed, and the opportunities it provided.

Farming, which was the chief occupation of the residents for decades, is seasonal work, with periods of leisure or light work. Of course, other states were agricultural, too, and the *opportunity* to write is not the performance. Something about the mixture of inhabitants and their interest in politics and religion turned them into a highly articulate people. If tragic themes are lacking in Indiana literature, so are cults of unintelligibility—that is, the obscure self-expressionists and the experimental schools and movements. Indiana had no synthetic literary center such as Greenwich Village or Sante Fe. Hoosiers wanted, above all, to communicate, to be understood by their contemporaries.

The absence of an adequate free school system for so long had three interesting effects. Folklore, largely brought in by Southerners, was orally preserved, embroidered, and disseminated, with less competition from superior literary authors. Even today Indiana is recognized as having a large body of folklore, collected and uncollected. Moreover, it is the home of the tall story. There was a recognized "liar's bench" in many towns, and the leading story teller was admired for his talent. Storytelling was a recognized form of social intercourse and entertainment. The best storytellers collected loyal audiences and elevated loafing to a fine art. The practice has disappeared fast since the introduction of the movie, the radio, and television, but the earlier Hoosiers sharpened their imaginations by perpetuating a great corpus of folklore.

The second effect was on the language. Archaisms of speech were retained, and colloquialisms developed, because there was no leveling and refining process provided by a standardized public school. Peculiarities of usage and pronunciation survived to enrich Hoosier speech. It is this speech that Riley appropriated and reported. Professor Robert Cordell of Purdue pointed out that Riley was never a dialect poet, because there was no real dialect in use in Indiana; rather, Riley utilized the uneducated Hoosier's bad grammar, as found in the central part of the state. Some critics argue that Hoosiers never spoke the way Riley wrote; but if that be true, as a generalization, Riley could always point to some one person he had heard speak that way. Left to his own resources for descriptions and comparisons, the Hoosier coined some apt and striking metaphors. He seemed to have what Aristotle called "an eye for resemblances," which is the very essence of expression. Some Indiana farmers today retain an original and graphic way of making comparisons.

The third effect of the paucity of schools was a hunger for knowledge that sought satisfaction through libraries and cultural or literary clubs. The Constitution of 1816 provided for county public libraries, and a majority opened them, then neglected them. Semiprivate libraries flourished better. Upon his death in 1840, William Maclure of New Harmony left $150,000 for the establishment of workingmen's libraries, and at least fifteen towns availed themselves of the bequest. Then, in 1852, the Indiana General Assembly provided for township school libraries, with books purchased from a state tax. More than two-thirds of the state's 938 townships secured libraries. Although the state appropriation was interrupted for ten years, the books already procured circulated furiously. Governor Tom Marshall attributed the literary fecundity of the state more to these libraries than to any other single cause. Early literary societies blossomed in Vevay, Vincennes, New Harmony, Bloomington, and Vernon. The Minerva of New Harmony, a second club founded by Robert Owen's granddaughter in 1859, is the oldest woman's club still to survive in Indiana, and it mothered many others.

There is also the factor of opportunity to publish. Artistic creation, as Levin Shucking points out in his little-known essay on *The Sociology of Literary Taste* (1923), is not necessarily something that erupts, forcing its way out, but is dependent to a large degree upon recognition and encouragement. The literary center of the first West was Lexington, Kentucky, where two stabs at issuing a literary periodical were made. Then Cincinnati assumed literary leadership, in more ways then one. It entertained such authors as Dickens, Mrs. Trollope, and Harriet Martineau, and also produced its own. Its publishing offices turned out books as well as periodicals. Starting in 1824, several magazines appeared, including James Hall's *Western Monthly Magazine,* which Professor Ralph L. Rusk calls the most important on the frontier. In 1841 the famous *Ladies' Repository* appeared and continued for the next thirty-five years. All of these periodicals invited contributions of poetry, essays, and moral fiction. Anthologies were another outlet. When W. T. Coggeshall issued his *Poets and Poetry of the West* at Columbus in 1860, he drew on 152 writers, of whom 36 were either natives or long-term residents of Indiana.

The period between the War of 1812 and the Civil War was the great era when men had limitless faith in their ability to improve society. Utopia was just around the corner. The cry for internal improvements activated the politicians, and Indiana embarked on a wild program in 1836. Proposed reforms bred organizations dedicated to promoting them. Along with others, Van Wyck Brooks has observed that "there is a vital connection between the phenomenon of literary energy and the phenomenon of human belief in the possibilities of the individual man."

Once a few Hoosiers began to achieve success in writing, momentum gathered rapidly because of the number of latent authors who simply needed the spur of an example. Some took up their pens to attack the picture of Hoosierdom presented by Edward Eggleston in 1871. A few tried to follow the pattern of historical fiction set by Lew Wallace in *The Fair God* (1873) and *Ben Hur* (1880). But it was James Whitcomb Riley who unloosed a horde of imitators, almost an industry. He is, of course, the writer most intimately and completely associated with Indiana. Born in Greenfield, in 1849, he quit school to become an itinerant sign-painter and wagon-show advertiser. He first gained notoriety by writing a poem in the Poe manner, signing it E.A.P., and submitting it in 1877 to a Kokomo paper as something found in an old dictionary. Some critics hailed it as a great addition to Poe literature, until Riley confessed his authorship. The *Indianapolis Journal* then hired him, and he frequently wrote verse for it. With a sensitive ear for Hoosier speech and a good eye for observation, he worked hard at polishing his lines. Still modest, he issued his first book, *The Old Swimmin' Hole and 'Leven More Poems,* under a pseudonym in 1883. The book immediately went into a second printing. Riley increased the popularity of his poems by traveling widely to give readings. Sometimes he appeared with the humorist Bill Nye, who did not find it so funny keeping Riley sober.

Few people today can recall that Riley was also a magnificent actor. When he called on friends or at his publisher's, he frequently assumed a role—an old farmer, a pious clergyman, a saloon keeper, or some such—and he would stay in character throughout his visit. Because he thought in rhyme, he entertained his cronies with impromptu verse suitable for the particular occasion. Once when he was staying at a resort hotel, where he had disgraced himself by some antic at dinner, he sat silently on the long porch next morning, sobering up. He could see the distant ladies in their rockers whispering among themselves and glancing his way. Finally he turned to his secretary-companion and said: *"They* think I'm sorry." [3]

Yale University conferred an honorary master's degree on Riley. The Lilly Library at Indiana University has his manuscripts and all his books in first editions. The Indiana Historical Society published a bibliography of his works. A children's hospital in Indianapolis is named for him. For all his wide and enduring popularity, his appeal is not well understood. It does not rest with children, for as Jeannette Covert Nolan, herself a writer for teenagers, perceptively pointed out, Riley is not primarily a poet for children. [4] Some youngsters don't care for his poems, and lines like "the Gobble-uns'll git you ef you don't watch out" [5] are a little bit frightening. Rather, she contended, he was a poet *about* childhood, *for* adults. He was one of the first authors to mine the rich vein of nostalgia for lost youth and to discover its universal attraction.

Riley's poems look deceptively easy to imitate. He seemed to demonstrate that an education was not necessary for writing, and that homely subjects were fit topics for poetry. All the stored-up observations of domestic life and nature were poured out in rustic bad verse by unsuspected harborers of the muse. Persons who might have developed their aptitude for music or painting turned to writing, instead, because they saw their friends doing it and because they seemed to feel that "If Jim Riley can make money writing poems like that, then, by golly, I can!" The urge was stimulated by a new crop of literary societies organized in the 1870s and 1880s, for men as well as women.

Another curious development was the organization of the

3. From conversations with D. Laurance Chambers, Eli Lilly, and Reginald Sullivan, all of whom knew Riley.

4. "Riley as a Children's Poet," in *Poet of the People: An Evaluation of James Whitcomb Riley,* by Jeannette Covert Nolan, Horace Gregory, and James T. Farrell (Bloomington: Indiana University Press, 1951).

5. From the poem "Little Orphant Annie," in *The Orphant Annie Book,* by James Whitcomb Riley (Indianapolis: The Bobbs-Merrill Co., 1908).

Western Association of Writers at Indianapolis in 1886. Although writers in other states were eligible for membership, the association was monopolized by Hoosiers. The group held annual meetings, and these gatherings of fifty to a hundred members became week-long literary festivals at a lake resort. Members read their own effusions and listened in turn to others. The association lasted about twenty years.

A final aspect of the literary surge was the venture of the Merrill, Meigs and Company bookstore of Indianapolis into publishing, with the second edition of Riley's first book. In 1885 the firm absorbed another bookstore and became the Bowen-Merrill Company, publishers as well as booksellers. In 1898 the name was changed to Bobbs-Merrill, and it became exclusively a publishing house in 1910. The existence of a publishing company in Indiana that could market its products nationally was a great stimulus to Indiana writers, and its employees kept an eye out for budding local authors. It was a Bowen-Merrill lawbook salesman who brought in a manuscript from a Shelbyville attorney named Charles Major. *When Knighthood Was in Flower* appeared in 1898 and became a best-seller for fourteen consecutive months. Riley remained a Bobbs-Merrill property, and Gene Stratton Porter started with them.

If Riley was the Hoosier favorite, Kin Hubbard was not far behind. Hubbard's cartoon creation of Abe Martin caused some ripples. Hubbard was a native of Ohio, from the hill country around Bellefontaine, where he was born in 1868. He had a good deal of experience as a silhouette artist, minstrel show organizer, vaudeville manager, and cartoonist before he settled in at the *Indianapolis News* in 1904 for the rest of his life. He first drew Abe Martin after the 1904 national election and identified him as a rustic philosopher from Brown County, Indiana's most rural county. A single-sentence commentary appeared under the one-column cut each day. Soon the feature was being syndicated in a growing number of papers. Hubbard's comments were better than his drawings. Fictitious friends of Abe appeared: Fawn Lippincut, Miss Tawny Apple, Lafe Budd, Constable Newt Plum, Tilford Moots, and Tell Binkley.

Meanwhile, the inhabitants of Brown County felt that they

were being ridiculed. At length they saw certain advantages in being identified with such a popular character and adopted him as their own. Annually, starting in 1907 and continuing until his death in 1930, Hubbard put together his cartoons and quips in book form. They sold widely, and reruns of his cartoons have appeared recently in newspapers. Abe Martin is now irrevocably considered a Hoosier type. When Indiana turned a piece of Brown County into a state park and built a hotel in it, the hotel was named the Abe Martin Lodge.

Here are some samples of Hubbard-Martin comments:

"It aint people's ignorance that causes so much trouble, it's ther bein' sure o' things that aint true."

"The first thing a feller does when he's held up is change his mind about what he used t' think he'd do."

"A feller never knows what he would o' done till he's been married a couple o' years."

"Lemmie Peters, who graduated with such high honors in June, is lookin' fer somethin' light an' remunerative."

"Look out fer th' feller who kin drive a car an' talk on any subject."

"Lafe Budd's mother-in-law is comin' to visit anyway."

"Once in a long while some feller retires from th' poultry business instead o' quittin'."

"I kin always tell a feller who has married a good housekeeper by th' way he brightens up when I speak kindly to him." [6]

Before his death in an auto accident in 1970, the late Herb Shriner of Fort Wayne gave promise on television of being Hubbard's heir. "I was born in Ohio," Shriner once explained, "but moved to Indiana as soon as I heard about it." He made other observations:

"We had a pretty fast bunch back home. Saturday night,

6. Frank McKinney Hubbard, *Abe Martin on Things in General* (Indianapolis: Abe Martin Publishing Co., 1925), unpaged; Hubbard, *Abe Martin's Barbed Wire* (Indianapolis: Bobbs-Merrill Co., 1928), pp. 17, 34; Hubbard, *Abe Martin's Town Pump* (Indianapolis: Bobbs-Merrill Co., 1929), pp. 110, 130, 183.

'twasn't nuthin for us to go down to the barbershop and watch a few haircuts.''

''Back home we had a beauty contest once. Nobody won.'' [7]

Indiana's most illustrious author was Booth Tarkington (1869–1946). Born in Indianapolis and reared in a comfortable middle-class family, Tarkington so thoroughly enjoyed his early life that he gave little promise of ever undertaking any serious occupation—certainly not so lonely and exacting a craft as writing. He enrolled at Purdue University, where he made the acquaintance of humorist George Ade and cartoonist John McCutcheon. After two years, he transferred to Princeton University, where he was active in student publications and dramatics. He wrote the first play produced by the Triangle Club. Returning home in 1893, he tried his hand at illustrating before concentrating on teaching himself to write. His first work was a historical novel that no one would publish, until later. His second was *The Gentleman from Indiana,* which S. S. McClure published in 1899, on the recommendation of Hamlin Garland. It became a best seller.

Tarkington married in 1902 and was elected to the state legislature, where he learned that he hated to speak in public. Novels followed in rapid succession, even during the two periods when he lived in Europe. He tried writing plays with Harry Leon Wilson; ultimately his *Clarence* (1919) was most successful. All the time, he was drinking too much, and his wife divorced him in 1911. He remarried late in the following year, and his second wife and his physician succeeded in persuading him to give up liquor. His novels grew more realistic. With *Penrod,* in 1914, Tarkington showed a real understanding of children and revealed considerable humor. *Penrod* was followed by *Seventeen.* In 1918 he published *The Magnificent Ambersons,* which won the Pulitzer Prize in fiction. He repeated that achievement in 1921 with *Alice Adams,* the story of an ambitious girl who tried—and failed—to win a wealthy husband by fabricating

7. Quoted in interview with Shriner's daughter, *Indianapolis Star,* September 8, 1975.

small lies about her family. Through the twenties, thirties, and early forties, he continued to turn out one popular novel after another, along with short stories.

Academic honors were conferred on Tarkington, and he was awarded the gold medal for fiction of the National Institute of Arts and Letters in 1933, and the Howells Medal of the American Academy of Arts and Letters in 1945. For many of the sixty-five books to his credit, he used the Indiana scene as settings. A bibliography of his works was published by the Indiana Historical Society in 1948.

After he had outgrown his romanticism, Tarkington wrote well of middle-class Americans and their affinity for economic success. He could be realistic without being naturalistic or bitter, and he reflected much social history of the first four decades of this century. He was good at creating a sense of time and place, and he exhibited a quiet optimism about humanity that is often interpreted as superficiality. If his characters are not always memorable, possibly it is because he stood a little apart from, and above, them. Yet he is an easy author to underestimate, because he handled the language so well and wrote so smoothly. Out of critical favor today, Tarkington undoubtedly will be rediscovered, even by those English professors who ignore him now.

Among literary critics, Theodore Dreiser (1871–1945) commands greater respect than Tarkington as a major American novelist. In contrast to Tarkington, Dreiser came out of a Catholic, Germanic, impoverished family. He was born in Terre Haute, started school there, but lived in several other Indiana towns. Dreiser graduated from Warsaw High School in 1887 and went to Chicago to find work. Two years later, with financial help and urging from a high school teacher, he attended Indiana University for a year. After his return to Chicago, he worked on newspapers and magazines. He lost his Catholic faith, but retained a prejudice against the British and the Jews. Turning to fiction, he produced *Sister Carrie* (1900), a realistic novel that sold less than five hundred copies until he republished it in 1907. Meanwhile, he had become a successful magazine editor in New York. In novel-writing, however, he sought to please only his own artistic conscience. Fired from his job for his pursuit of young girls, he left his wife and wrote four novels between 1911 and 1915. *Jennie Gerhardt* (1911) was another study of a young girl seeking love in a city and was more carefully written than *Sister Carrie,* which went into a third edition prompted by the second book's success. Concerned with presenting the conflict between individual desires and the conventions of society, Dreiser insisted that there were firm social classes in the United States and that that structure heavily affected individuals. *The Financier* (1912) was perhaps the best novel about an American businessman up to that time.

Censorship and literary criticism plagued him, but did not deter him from his goal of telling the truth as he saw it. Dreiser enjoyed attacking current moral standards and asking embarrassing questions about life. His stand influenced several younger writers. In telling the story of a socially ambitious young man who killed his pregnant girl friend because of twisted values, Dreiser produced *An American Tragedy* (1925). He lent himself to Communist causes in the 1930s and eventually married his long-time mistress. Unlike Tarkington, Dreiser was not proudly claimed by Indiana. He wrote specifically about his birthplace in *A Hoosier Holiday* (1916) and *Dawn* (1931), disparaging his family and the small towns where he lived.

The momentum of Indiana literary production appears to have slackened since the end of World War II, even though the number of authors has increased since 1916. Admittedly, more college professors have published than ever before. What Hoosiers have to say, however, has not caught a national audience, as it used to. The regional periodicals are gone or have become academic. Competition from auto travel and television has diminished the audience. Tastes have changed. A noticeable amount of ancestor worship prevails among readers; the two houses in which Riley lived and Gene Stratton Porter's two sylvan retreats are preserved as memorials, and the former homes of Eggleston, Wallace, Moody, Ade, Pyle, and Tarkington are pointed out to visitors.

As for art, there may have been as many painters in Indiana as writers, but the number who supported themselves by selling their pictures was a good deal lower than the number of successful authors. Art on the frontier seemed to begin with sign-painting. If the practitioner had any talent, he would soon try painting portraits. Before or after that bold step, he might study with an established artist and be instructed. Later on, he might even use a camera to obtain a more accurate likeness, then paint over it. The first art school did not open in Indiana until 1878. A few good artists came here to settle or grew up here; others migrated from Indiana to pursue careers elsewhere. The travelers or short-term visitors hardly count, even though they produced some of the best early pictures of Indiana scenes.

Jacob Cox, a tinsmith from Pittsburgh, made Indianapolis his home in 1832 and remained until his death in 1892. Without formal training, Cox simply had an overpowering desire to draw and paint, and he taught himself. Opening a studio in 1840, he first painted a banner for the Indianapolis delegation that attended the rally at Tippecanoe Battleground for William Henry Harrison, but his real vocation became portraiture. He grew better and better as an artist and painted six governors. At age fifty, he enrolled in a New York art school for a few months and then returned to Indianapolis. Although limited in his handling of paint, he was highly regarded, and many young men and women studied under his supervision. The Indianapolis Art Museum has two of his portraits and several of his landscapes.

His contemporary, George W. Morrison, born in Baltimore, migrated to New Albany in 1840 and set up as a professional painter. For the next fifty-three years, until his death, Morrison was the city's chief resident artist. Evidently he was trained, as he was technically competent and did many portraits, including one governor.

Another artist of the same period—George Winter—worked at Logansport and Lafeyette. Winter was a transplanted Englishman who came West, first of all, to paint Indians in 1836. Unlike Cox and Morrison, he had received training in New York. He made watercolor portraits of numerous individual

Miami and Potawatomi and scenes of their homes. His most noted portrait was of Frances Slocum and her two daughters, after she was identified as a white captive taken from Pennsylvania in 1778 as a child. Winter settled in Logansport and painted landscapes, as well as portraits. In 1851 he moved to Lafayette, a larger town, and made a good living with his brush. He died there in 1876. His works hang in several museums. Through a publication in 1948 of the Indiana Historical Society, *The Journals and Indian Paintings of George Winter, 1837–1839,* he has become better known throughout the state and beyond.

In the post-Civil War period, four more artists came to prominence. William M. Chase of Nineveh began his painting career as a youth in Indianapolis during and after the war, but after study in Munich, he settled in New York in 1878. His reputation is national in scope, and he had many pupils. James F. Gookins of Terre Haute trained here and abroad. He was a portrait and landscape artist active in Indianapolis and in his home city until 1889. Joseph H. Dille, without formal training, did most of his work in Fort Wayne, moved to Goshen for eight years, then back to Fort Wayne from 1877 to 1910. Self-taught Barton S. Hays began painting in Attica, then practiced in Indianapolis from 1858 to 1882, before moving to Minnesota.

At the turn of the century, John E. Bundy was painting landscapes around Richmond, from 1890 to 1933. He had grown up in Morgan County and developed his talent in Monrovia and Martinsville. J. Ottis Adams of Amity studied in London and Munich. He painted portraits and landscapes in Muncie and Fort Wayne until 1904, when he moved to Indianapolis and then to Brookville. William J. Forsyth also studied in Munich and then returned to Indianapolis in 1888, where he remained until his death in 1935. In a similar career, Otto Stark (1859–1926) of Indianapolis studied art in Cincinnati, New York, and Paris, and settled for a few years in New York in 1887. Then he returned to Indianapolis to teach at Manual Training High School and to paint landscapes and romantic urban scenes. Theodore C. Steele, another native who studied in Munich, returned to Indianapolis in 1885, but moved to Brown County in 1907 for notable landscape work. He died in 1928, and his studio home is preserved as a state memorial.

Steele's move to the scenic grandeur of Brown County marked the beginning of an artists' colony there. Landscape painters in particular found the hills and hollows, ever changing in the four seasons, a challenge. Some of them settled there, others came for a season. They were infected by Munich's interest in regional art, focusing their interest on Indiana. Steele and occasional companions tramped about the state for appealing views.

Meanwhile, the Art Association of Indianapolis had been founded in 1883 by May Wright Sewall. It sponsored exhibitions and opened a short-lived art school. Then, in 1895, the association received a large bequest from John Herron, an Englishman who had come to Indiana in 1847 and to Indianapolis in 1883. Herron inherited modest wealth and made money in real estate. His will was contested, and the association did not receive the money immediately. It amounted to $225,000, and with it they opened another art school in January 1902 and built a museum and new school (1906–1908), called the John Herron Art Institute. Exhibitions of Indiana artists with prizes started in 1905. Later a Hoosier Salon Patrons Association sponsored shows in Chicago for Indiana artists. They were moved to Indianapolis in 1941. The annual Hoosier Salon continues, and a permanent gallery offers pictures the year round.

Richmond had an art association in 1897 that encouraged local artists with annual exhibitions and traveling shows to other state cities. A local colony of artists there grouped themselves around John S. Bundy. Muncie developed a group of resident artists, and so did South Bend. To promote the artists identified with Brown County, the Brown County Art Gallery Association was formed in Nashville, Indiana, in 1926 and still offers the works of state artists for sale. A rival group, the Brown County Art Guild, broke off in the 1950s and maintains a gallery in Nashville also. These artists may also show at the Hoosier Salon in Indianapolis.

The biennial Indiana Artists Show, held at the John Herron

Art Museum in Indianapolis, offers pictures and sculpture that have been selected by an outside jury. It considers itself superior to what may be seen at Nashville or at the Hoosier Salon and gives recognition to the most modern art. Yet the Brown County artists sell steadily. A very few artists, such as Steele, Goth, and Bohm, have made both shows. Wilbur Peat, director of the Herron Museum for thirty-six years, wrote two invaluable books on Indiana artists and architects. The art school still carries the Herron name, but the museum continues today as the Indianapolis Museum of Art.

The best modern artists that Indiana claims would include Wayman Adams (1883–1959), one of the country's finest portraitists. Adams was born in Muncie, studied at the John Herron Art School, and went to Italy to work under William M. Chase. Upon his return, he opened a studio in Indianapolis and displayed great influence in the state. Then, like Chase, he moved to New York. Victor Higgins (1884–1949) was born in Shelbyville, but went to Chicago in 1899 to study at the Art Institute. He was in Europe for about four years before the outbreak of war, and upon his return settled in Taos, New Mexico, where he spent the rest of his life. Higgins's oils and watercolors of southwestern scenes and Indians have made him a significant interpreter. Clifton Wheeler (1883–1953) studied with Will Forsythe and William M. Chase. Wheeler opened a studio in Indianapolis in 1911 and taught at the John Herron Art School. Like Steele, he painted a number of attractive local landscapes.

Marie Goth (1887–1975) was a native of Indianapolis who studied with Otto Stark and several eastern artists. She settled in Brown County about 1924 and soon became the acknowledged leader of the art colony. She understood color and was skillful in design. She did a variety of pictures, including many portraits. Another Brown County artist of superior ability was C. Curry Bohm (1894–1971), whose landscapes have gone into museums as well as private homes. Bohm studied at the Chicago Art Institute, started making annual visits to Brown County in 1920, and settled permanently in Nashville, Indiana, ten years later.

Donald Mattison (1905–1975) was director of the John Herron Art School from 1933 until his retirement in 1970. Mattison found time to paint portraits and American scenes. Floyd Hopper, a graduate of the John Herron Art School, spent a summer at the Pennsylvania Academy of Fine Arts. He began painting landscapes in the 1930s. A teacher of art himself, Hopper became one of the leading watercolorists in the Middle West. His contrasts of strong colors identify many of his works. Living in the country near Noblesville, he continues to win prizes. Four active artists are teaching at Indiana-Purdue University's Herron Art School: James McGarrel, Rudy Pozzatti, Edmund Brucker, and Harry A. Davis. Garro Antresian is a former faculty member who now teaches at the University of New Mexico.

The landscape artists have painted primarily the Indiana scene. They have found it beautiful and have tried to preserve it on canvas or paper, especially those attached to Brown County. A few artists who left Indiana cannot be identified as Hoosiers by their works.

Indiana is not the home of a school of painting. Its artists, until very recent exceptions, have been popular rather than innovative. The best are very good, but not great. The same might be said of its writers. At their own levels, both groups have found wide audiences, and their reception has satisfied most Hoosier authors and artists.

In 1965 the children of J. K. Lilly, Jr., gave his estate, Oldfields, to the Art Association of Indianapolis. Oldfields consisted of forty-five acres rising from the White River valley and running along Thirty-eighth Street and Northwestern Avenue. Included was the stately house and its period furnishings, which now comprise the Lilly Pavilion of the Decorative Arts. A new museum, built through the generosity of Mr. and Mrs. Herman C. Krannert of Indianapolis and called the Krannert Pavilion, houses the pictures transferred from the Herron Art Museum in 1970. Then the Clowes Pavilion was added by the sons of Dr. and Mrs. G. H. A. Clowes, to hold that family's notable collection of medieval and renaissance art. Adjoining that complex is the Grace Showalter Pavilion of the Performing Arts, which is the new home of the civic theater, the Booth Tarkington

Players. Altogether, these resources are called the Indianapolis Museum of Art. The John Herron Art School was taken over in 1967 by the Indiana and Purdue Universities Center in Indianapolis as its art school. Art museums are not ranked according to the quality of their holdings, but in relation to the size of the metropolitan area served. The Indianapolis Museum has a larger percentage of attendance than any other museum in the country.

An Indiana Arts Commission was created in 1969 and, with federal grants and local funds, has acted to take painting, music, ballet, theater, and poetry into various communities. It has an over-all purpose of giving enough recognition to local talent to persuade artists to remain in Indiana. A similar organization, the Metropolitan Arts Council in Indianapolis, founded in 1966, advises artists on finding customers and aids businesses in selecting Indiana art for their offices or for temporary public display. The council has seventeen artists on salary who demonstrate or perform in schools and colleges. Now there are about forty art councils in other Indiana cities.

No account of community art projects can omit mention of the modern architecture to be found in Columbus. The movement began in 1942, with completion of a new First Christian Church in contemporary geometric design by Eliel Saarinen. After the war, the Cummins Engine Foundation offered to pay architectural fees for new schools if the school board would select an architect from a short list submitted by a panel of the country's most distinguished architects. No architect was to design more than one building. A dozen schools have been built under this arrangement. In addition, the foundation has furnished the architectural fee for a new post office, a fire station, a retirement center, a mental health consulting center, and a golf clubhouse.

The primary instigator of this architectural program is J. Irwin Miller, head of the Cummins Engine Company. Miller's action stimulated churches, banks, businesses, the library board, the newspaper, and other philanthropists to undertake the building of structures of modern design. With federal funds, a quarter of the Columbus downtown area was cleared and is being rebuilt. A two-block square was made into a covered shopping mall containing a public commons (two theaters, a restaurant, exhibit hall, playground, and meeting rooms), a gift of Mr. and Mrs. Miller and his sister. Elsewhere, a number of Victorian store fronts have been renovated and restored. The whole city has grown conscious of good design, and it attracts visitors from all over the country. They are all surprised that such sophisticated architectural development should occur in Indiana, in a city of 30,000.

8

Hoosier Madness

$\mathcal{A}$S closely as the Kentucky Derby is identified with Kentucky, so the Indianapolis 500—an annual 500-mile automobile racing marathon—is identified with Indiana—and the present owner of the Indianapolis Motor Speedway intends to keep it that way.

The two-and-a-half-mile rectangular track was conceived as a means of promoting public acceptance of the automobile. The race was originally to publicize durability and hence dependability of motorcars. The idea belonged to Carl G. Fisher of Indianapolis, who owned an auto agency and was an inveterate competitive racer—first, of bicycles, then of balloons and cars. In 1904 Fisher entered into partnership with James A. Allison to manufacture a carbide gas lamp they called "Prest-O-Lite," which all the burgeoning auto manufacturers soon wanted to use. Thirteen years later, they sold the company to Union Carbide and Carbon Corporation for $9 million.

The creation of an outdoor laboratory as a testing ground for cars was begun by Fisher in 1908, with the acquisition of farm acreage on the west side of Indianapolis. He talked Allison into joining him, and they invited two local friends in as investment partners: Arthur C. Newby, president of National Motor Car Company, and Frank H. Wheeler, manufacturer of the Wheeler-Schebler carburetor. Fisher's indispensable talent was for promotion. Naturally competitive, he believed that racing was the best way of comparing the merits of various cars, and he knew that racing would bring out paying crowds. The first track was made of tar and crushed stone, which not only shredded tires but developed chuck holes and threw up clouds of dust in the races of 1909. The track had to be paved if racing was to continue, and Fisher insisted on bricks, a further heavy investment to be added to the cost of the grandstands the partners had constructed.

The first five-hundred-mile race was scheduled for 1911. A twenty-four-hour event or a thousand-mile race would last too long to attract an audience, Fisher decided, but a five-hundred-mile race, running about seven hours, seemed just right. Fisher insisted on $25,000 in prize money, much higher than any other race offered. He was adept at stimulating the auto manufacturers and the tire companies to test their products in such a race. Much shorter races had been run on dirt tracks of state fairgrounds, but a long race, he argued, would be a real test of performance. The glory of winning would help sell a lot of cars.

The Marmon Company of Indianapolis employed an engineer who was also a racer, Ray Harroun. The company built a new car for the 1911 Memorial Day race and persuaded Harroun to drive it. From experience, Harroun knew that no car could be driven wide open for five hundred miles without some mechanical failure or numerous tire replacements. Most of the forty cars entered were riding Michelin or Firestone tires. Harroun figured that a steady pace of seventy-five miles an hour would not strain the engine or require more than two tire changes; whereas a speed of seventy-eight miles per hour would wear his tires in one hour. His calculations proved correct. Before a crowd of 80,000, Harroun kept doggedly at his pace. Other cars passed him, but burned up their rubber and had to stop for extra tire changes. More cars dropped out with mechanical trouble. Harroun gave way to a relief driver on his first tire change, then took back the wheel on the second stop. He was now running in second place; but with nineteen laps to go, the lead car, running at eighty miles per hour, had to stop for new tires, and Harroun breezed under the checkered flag after six hours and forty-two minutes. His average speed was 74.59 miles per hour.

The other cars were two-seaters, and a mechanic rode beside the driver. One of his duties was to keep looking behind so as to advise the driver whether another car was pulling up beside him. Harroun's Marmon had room for only one, and there were murmurs that such a car was less safe in a race. Harroun took care of that objection by fastening a mirror on the cowl— the first rear-vision mirror ever used on a car.

At other times during the year, the track was used for testing cars and tires, but the annual five-hundred-mile race at Indianapolis was the indisputable climax in racing. Prize money was raised to $50,000. The cars were actually regular engines in stripped-down or streamlined bodies, so that the winner would be advertised as a car of durability and high performance. Simply to finish the five hundred miles was an achievement. It was not long, however, before special engines were built for racing. The Duesenberg brothers in Indianapolis were more interested in designing efficient motors before they built passenger cars. Out in Los Angeles, Harry Miller, a carburetion expert, began turning out racing engines in 1914. He employed Fred Offenhauser, who bought the shop in 1932 and made the reliable four-cylinder "Offy." The Chevrolet brothers—Louis, Arthur, and Gaston—were an early racing team for Buick and built a special racer in 1916. The Speedway Company ordered special race cars of its own. Entries were limited to thirty-three cars.

Fisher was also beating the drums for improved roads, declaring that they were a key to greater car sales. He advocated a coast-to-coast highway. In 1913 he left Indianapolis with a caravan of cars, called the Trail Blazers, for the Pacific Coast. It took them almost a month to cover the distance. Fisher suggested calling the proposed road the Lincoln Highway. It was not completed until fifteen years later.

The annual Memorial Day races grew faster, of course, but had not reached an average of ninety miles per hour by 1916, when racing was suspended the next year because of the war. Fisher, meanwhile, had bought part of a mangrove swamp on a peninsula opposite Miami, Florida. He grew more interested in reclaiming the swamp, which he developed into Miami Beach. T. E. "Pop" Myers, a realtor whom Fisher put in charge of the ticket office, became general manager of the Speedway in 1916. The next year, Wheeler sold his interest to Allison, who turned to making aircraft engines in the war.

When racing resumed in 1919, speeds picked up. The next year, a group of Indianapolis businessmen started offering lap prizes. Pete DePaolo averaged 101 miles per hour in 1925 and cut the race time to just under five hours. That speed was not surpassed until 1932. The Cummins Engine Company of Columbus, Indiana, entered a diesel-powered car in 1931 that went the full 500 miles, Dale Evans driving, without a stop, but the car finished thirteenth. It proved at least the durability of that type of engine. Regulations affecting the size of engines changed frequently. Superchargers were first used in 1924, and the first front-wheel-drive car was entered. Balloon tires were used in 1925, eliminating one tire change, and all the cars had wire wheels in 1927. In that year, too, Fisher, Allison, and Newby sold the speedway to Captain Eddie Rickenbacker, famed World War I aviator and previously a race driver. Rickenbacker found financial backing in Detroit and added a golf course. Racing continued through 1941, with Lou Meyer and Wilbur Shaw each winning three times. The winning speed reached 117 miles per hour in 1938, and there were no more riding mechanics. Prize money from the speedway, from accessory makers, and from lap awards reached $90,000 and over.

Again war interrupted the annual event. Grass grew among the bricks, weeds surrounded the garages, and the grandstands were beaten by weather. Rickenbacker had lost interest, and Wilbur Shaw was the most concerned about reviving the race. He talked to Rickenbacker and learned his selling price. Then he approached Anton Hulman, Jr., of Terre Haute, a former Yale athlete, a wealthy wholesale grocer, and a sportsman who took pride in "the greatest spectacle in racing" at Indianapolis. Hulman bought the speedway in 1945 and made Shaw president and general manager. The new owner did not expect to make money from the race, but hoped to be able to pay the cost of the new grandstands and repaving the track. Likewise, he found it necessary to raise the total prize money.

The Memorial Day classic was resumed in 1946. The last winner before the track closed during World War II had been Mauri Rose of South Bend. Rose came back to win again in 1947 and 1948. The 1949 race was televised locally and the cameras gave such good coverage that the speedway declined to continue such a show for free viewing. It was made available later via closed circuit to theaters and for delayed showing on network television. The average speed increased to 130 miles per hour in 1954 under Bill Vukovich, who was killed in the following year's race. Wilbur Shaw died in a plane crash in 1954, and since that time Hulman has served as president. Suddenly, in 1955, the American Automobile Association abolished its Contest Board, which had supervised and regulated each running of the Indy 500. Hulman called together all interested parties and helped form the U.S. Auto Club to conduct automotive competitions and tests of every kind. He also repaved the track with asphalt.

The Miller-Offenhauser plant in California had been purchased in 1946 by Lou Meyer and Dale Drake. Their engines were used in a number of race cars, along with cars produced by A. J. Watson. Lew Welch of Michigan entered a front-wheel-drive car in 1946 built by Bud and Ed Winfield. Called a Novi, the automobile was sensationally fast but did not finish. Cummins tried again with diesel-powered cars. Then, in 1957, George Salin modified a Meyer-Drake engine to run on its side, thus lowering the center of gravity. Driven by Sam Hanks, the car won. Another tilted engine won the following year, and horizontals seemed to be the thing, although Watson's upright engine won in 1959 and 1960. Later cars mounted the engine in the rear so that its height was not a factor in front-end design.

Beginning in 1957, the race became part of a three-day festival, sponsored by an organization of Indianapolis businessmen. A golf tournament was scheduled, there was a mayor's breakfast, a governor's ball, the inevitable Speedway Queen and street parade; and on race day, there appeared a profusion of college and high school bands, a military color guard, visiting celebrities, with the release of thousands of balloons. A motel and a racing museum were added to the facilities.

Speeds continued to rise. In 1967 A. J. Foyt became a three-time winner with an average speed of 151 miles per hour, a figure that had seemed mythical twenty years earlier. A qualifying lap of almost 170 miles per hour had been set by Mario Andretti, who barely edged out Parnelli Jones driving a turbine engine. Complaints about unfair competition between turbine and piston engines resulted in prohibition of anything but severely modified turbine engines. The total purse was more than $734,000, with Foyt taking $171,000. Race time had been reduced to three and a half hours, contrasted to the 1911 time of six and three-quarters hours.

In 1976 no car qualified at less than 180 miles per hour, and Johnny Rutherford, who won the pole position in a McLaren-turbo-Offy car, turned a lap at 190 miles per hour, and so did Mario Andretti in a similar car a few days later. Rutherford went on to win the race, cut to 255 miles by rain, and carried off $256,000 in prizes. Racing for the nineteenth time, A. J. Foyt came in second.

The record speed for the full five hundred miles was set in 1972 by Mark Donahue in another McLaren-built car at just a shade under 163 miles per hour. Since 1969 total prize money has exceeded a million dollars. It is this plain bread-and-butter appeal, plus the unparalleled crowd (238,000 reserved seats plus about 70,000 in the infield) that keeps the Indianapolis 500 far and away the greatest spectacle in racing. There are two other 500-mile races now, at Ontario, California, and Mount Pocono, Pennsylvania, but they are much smaller in prize money and crowds. The entire track at Indianapolis was repaved in 1976, and the elusive 200 miles per hour in qualifying is not out of reach.

A lot of folklore has grown up about the technological benefits of the race to the manufacture of cars. The first rear-vision mirror is cited as an example, but Harroun's application of 1911 was not adopted by the auto industry until a decade later. It is true that Rickenbacker told Floyd Clymer in 1946 that "approximately 70 percent of all the mechanical improvements that went into the private automobile were originated on the Indianapolis Speedway, or at least perfected there." [1] That is pardonable exaggeration. Academic professors of mechanical engineering frankly doubt that sweeping statement. High-compression engines, fuel-injector systems, overhead camshafts, hydraulic brakes, superchargers, shock absorbers, turbo chargers, fuel mixtures, Firestone and Goodyear tires have all been used on race cars. Early auto companies did use the speedway for testing their cars, on race day and other days; but, as they consolidated and grew bigger, they developed their own proving grounds and laboratories in the 1920s. Some testing of parts by parts companies and of tires at the speedway goes on today.

The social history of the 500-mile race is not as exciting as the race itself, yet it is revealing. Some Hoosiers did not regard kindly the "desecration" of Memorial Day by a sporting event. Indeed, the state legislature was induced to pass an act in 1923 to prohibit such commercialized sports on Memorial Day, but the governor vetoed it. Resentment continued in some quarters for another twenty-five years, despite all the newspaper publicity, as the race was blamed for the decline and disappearance of a Memorial Day parade in Indianapolis. Indeed, in other towns the annual parade to a cemetery in May continues as a stout tradition.

As late as the late 1940s, the "old society" of Indianapolis ignored the race. The crowds were regarded as vulgar invaders who made many streets impassable. Race drivers were considered in the same class as jockeys by those who looked down upon both groups. But in the postwar years the rise of a newly affluent society that began to plan entertainments around the "500" weekend changed the acceptance of the race. Wilbur

1. Joseph Floyd Clymer, *Indianapolis Race History* (Los Angeles: n.p., 1946), p. 2.

Shaw was seen to be a modest, well-mannered businessman, and Tony Hulman, of course, was of impeccable social standing in Terre Haute. Some drivers were perceived to be men with considerable knowledge of mechanical engineering, not just heavy-footed daredevils. While a small old guard lamented the passing of the traditional Memorial Day observance in favor of a hedonistic festival, a growing Indianapolis society embraced the 500 as a peak in the late social season. It became an event to capture a visiting celebrity for lunch or dinner. Conquest of the city by the race is now complete.

If the speedway stimulated auto manufacturers, why didn't that industry grow up in Indianapolis, rather than Detroit? If it had, everyone would have credited the race as a cause. The answer may be, not that the Detroit environment was better, but that certain manufacturing geniuses rose in Michigan who were not matched by those in Indiana. Henry Ford, Walter Chrysler, the Dodge brothers, Henry Joy, Billy Durant, Alvan Macauley knew how to manage a growing business enterprise, as well as build cars. They understood the importance of a network of local dealers and knew the features in a car that would appeal to families. Further, while Studebaker sought to build family cars, Stutz, Duesenberg, Marmon, National and Premier allowed themselves to be distracted at first by designing and building race cars, rather than concentrating on what families wanted and could afford. Speed meant little in a family car, since early roads would not permit it, and it was not the only measure of durability. Carl Fisher missed his guess there, but he brought fame to Indianapolis.

The craze for basketball in Indiana is quite different from the Indy 500, although the state basketball tournament began the same year as the race. Basketball is not a single competition, but a season of several months. High school competition pervades the whole state and involves local youths exclusively. It is completely amateur and noncommercial. Success depends on nothing mechanical, just the ability to handle a ball and toss it through an iron hoop. Indiana high school teams do it superbly well. Hoosiers love the game and have no trouble justifying the emphasis on it in high school or college.

Because there are many more high schools than colleges, the madness centers on the former, with an overflow of enthusiasm for college basketball that does not extend to professional basketball. The school game is centered in each of several hundred communities as a focal point. High school teams play neighboring school teams, as they do in every state, but Indiana runs its annual tournament in somewhat different fashion. High schools are classed *A* to *D,* according to enrollment, and play other schools in their class; but at the end of the season, classifications are forgotten, and winners play winners, in progression, regardless of the school's size. It is a jubilant free-for-all.

The statewide tournament was organized in 1911 by the Booster Club of Indiana University. Then the Indiana High School Athletic Association stepped in to sponsor the next tournament and all those since that time. The final games were played at the Indiana University gymnasium through 1918. They were moved to Purdue University in 1919, and then to Indianapolis as a more central location in 1920. Eventually the Butler University Field House, seating 15,000, became the home of the finals. In 1974 the final games were moved to Indianapolis's new Market Street Arena, which holds 18,000.

In 1959, 712 high schools participated in the tournament; but through consolidations, barely 400 were involved in 1976. Eliminations begin early in March, with sectional contests. Newspapers give special attention to them, and the fever begins to rise. Sixty-four sectional winners emerge. Following that, the regional tournaments are played, which produce sixteen winning teams. The "sweet sixteen" then move, the following week, to the semifinals, or semistate tournament, that leaves the elite four winners. On the last Saturday in March, the four school teams meet in Indianapolis. They are paired in the afternoon, and the two winners play again in delirious competition that night.

In 1949 a state School Study Commission issued *An Evaluation of the Indiana Public Schools* and clucked its concern over basketball.

Competitive athletics, particularly basketball, hold the most favored place in the activity program of all schools. This overbalance is evidenced by proportion of staff time devoted to direction, the building facilities and equipment for that purpose, and by the community interest and concern for that one activity. The result of this overbalance is the impoverished condition of other types of activities with respect to the availability of pupils, the adequacy of financial support, and the relative values of educative experiences as evidenced by the supporting public.[2]

True, but the commission might as well have saved its breath. It overlooked one aspect of athletics in the high school program: they promote and give exercise as well to the high school band, to squads of cheer leaders, and to baton twirlers. It underestimated the social value of basketball in unifying a community. Regardless of politics, religion, or educational levels, everyone can rally around the high school team. The state championship is proudly added to the city limits signs. Even small towns tax themselves to build gymnasiums as big as or bigger than the high schools' academic buildings, and many rival college gyms. All winter long, perfectly sedate and cultured couples turn out to cheer the local team. Members of a winning team receive recognition and praise that inspire them with a warm feeling for their home town. They don't know what alienation means. Further, a winning team is often a passport to college with a rich scholarship.

The semifinals and the finals are the talk of the towns whose teams participate. Parents and other adults, to say nothing of classmates, descend on Indianapolis in droves, and residents of the capital city snap up all other available tickets. They see some extraordinary basketball. Crawfordsville High School won the first state tournament and has never repeated. Other high schools have. Muncie Central has won five times, and Frankfort four times. Nine have won the championship three times. They have been city schools, except for Martinsville, a town of about 4,700—which built a gymnasium seating 5,000 during the

2. Indiana, State Board of Education, School Study Commission, *An Evaluation of the Indiana Public Schools* (Indiana, 1949), p. 106.

period of its triple crowns. An Indianapolis high school did not win until 1955, and it was Crispus Attucks, which also won the next year and three years later.

The small high schools have provided some of the most memorable games. Jasper, a town of 5,200 with a high school enrollment of 400, started tournament play in 1949, after an undistinguished season of eleven victories and nine losses. But the team found itself and kept going, beating teams from comparable towns in the sectionals and regional. Then, in the semifinals, it put away Bedford and sneaked past Bloomington by one point. So it came to the finals, passing Auburn by five points. In the last game, with Madison, although an opposing player set a new individual scoring record of thirty-six points, Jasper persisted and again won a hair-raising game by one point.

There was nothing like it again until 1954, when little Milan, with a high school enrollment of 161, found itself in the semifinals facing Indianapolis Attucks—and left them behind. Then, in the finals, it polished off big Terre Haute Gerstmeyer and came up against Muncie Central, a school with an enrollment of 1,875. With the score at thirty to thirty, and five seconds to play, a Milan boy flipped the ball through the hoop without its touching the rim. Just a swish of the net, and it was all over, thirty-two to thirty. The town of Milan had been virtually vacated that day, and the returning caravan of cars lighted up the community in celebration early Sunday morning. It was a memorable experience for everybody and is remembered today.

Hoosiers readily admit their "madness" over basketball. They offer no apologies. It seems a natural disease, and they exhibit a capacity to enjoy without analysis. And the young people, too, display an enviable capacity to be and accept what they are: young people, free of social responsibilities for a while, reveling in their youth, their games, the furious activity and the heady excitement of it all. They remember the basketball seasons of which they were a part for the rest of their lives.

High school principals and superintendents have some reservations about the tournament. For every winner in the month-long eliminations, there are three losers. The pressures on players and coaches are severe, almost unbearable. Overdoing it was the creation of a high school basketball Hall of Fame in 1962. Nevertheless, the Indiana High School Athletic Association started a football tournament in 1973, although that game is still played by three classes of schools—big, middle-sized, and small. The three finals are held at host schools around the state, according to formula. Further, a basketball tournament for girls' teams was instituted in 1976 with entries from 360 high schools. The first state championship was won by Warsaw High School.

What has been the effect, if any, of 500-mile race activity and the basketball tournament? One is tempted to say that the focus of interest on these contests has indirectly prevented professional athletic teams in Indiana from achieving anything beyond a modest and uncertain success. Directly, the effect is different. They emphasize competition and the essential rightness of competing. It is a way of measuring effort and success. Alternatives for achievement are not clear. Individual competition seems natural, and the results are accepted. The race has not resulted in any widespread desire among Indiana boys to become auto mechanics or designers or race drivers. But they catch the spirit of intense competition even at the risk of life. They see that here is something that matters vitally to some people.

High school athletics touch them more intimately. Kids grow up knowing they must compete, that winning means excelling others. They see nothing wrong with that; if you don't make the first team, you're a substitute, or at least an enthusiastic fan. If you're a quitter or a sour-face, jealous of those with greater ability, that is nothing admirable. They learn the importance of perseverance because they repeatedly see the "sure winner" overtaken in the last minute by the "also ran." They learn that victory cannot be certain until the last whistle blows or the checkered flag drops. Until that final moment, you always have a chance to win. Transferred to other activities or a vocation, the same desire to excel prevails. Winning is great, but so is participation, because it calls out your best. Beneath contempt is feeling sorry for one's self. Small wonder that individualism persists in Indiana.

9

Summing Up

ARE Hoosiers today as distinctive from other Americans as they were? If not, when were they most distinguishable? And what are they now?

Indiana, in the middle of the eighteenth century, contained Indians, Frenchmen, and Negroes. Then came Anglo-Americans, a trickle at first that grew to a steady torrent. Although these new arrivals were from the South and the East, and sectional feelings colored their difference of outlook, they forged a new life in a new state and absorbed a modest number of foreign-born. By the time of the Civil War, Hoosiers were an identifiable lot. Travelers, visitors, and newcomers readily noticed certain traits. Hoosiers were self-reliant, self-assured, attached to the land, and used to hard work. But so were a lot of the inhabitants of other western areas. More distinctively, Hoosiers were known for their hospitable friendliness, their treatment of one another as equals, their good humor, and their shrewdness in judging character. Dependent as farmers were on weather, they committed themselves to Providence with humility and hope. Specifically, at that time, Hoosiers detested slavery, Negroes, state indebtedness, drunkenness, laziness, and horse thieves. They were mildly suspicious of Catholics, foreigners, public schools, and government interference in local affairs. They were indifferent to the political rights of women (in common with many citizens of other states) and to higher education at state expense. They supported state care of the needy and the growth of manufacturing. Optimistic, they were already boosters of their state's future.

After the shock of the Civil War, Hoosiers continued their rural life, participated intensively in politics, tolerated corrupt practices, saw fewer European immigrants than most other states, encouraged factories, and grew increasingly self-conscious of their own typicalness. Looking back from 1926, Mark Sullivan observed in *Our Times* that the typical American of 1900 more nearly resembled a Hoosier than he did the inhabitant of any other state. Surveying 1900 contemporaneously, Meredith Nicholson said that "Indiana has always lain near the currents of national life." It is strange that Hoosiers settled for typicality, as if they relished being average, rather than reaching for superiority. Possibly it was that typicalness that encouraged intolerance: for if I consider myself typical, then you who are different from me must be atypical—that is, radical or reactionary, perhaps inferior, not to be admired but ignored or opposed. It seemed appropriate that the center of population in the United States was located in southern Indiana in 1890, and in its slow westward course remained within the state until after 1940, longer than in any other state. It contributed to the self-appraisal that Hoosiers must be average.

Without boundary barriers and stretched between Lake Michigan and the Ohio, Indiana was athwart the main routes by which the East filled up the great West, making the state a constant witness to that national expansion, or manifest destiny. The state has never been plundered by outsiders, carpet-baggers who came in to mine or cut timber and then move on. What wealth and power were acquired were acquired by natives; usually by natives who were poor or middle-class to begin with.

From a retrospectus of Indiana's history one cannot help feeling that Hoosiers were most distinctively their own people in the period from 1900 to 1920. They were rural in background and outlook, without being rustic or uncouth. By then they were pleasantly mature but not sophisticated or urbane. They read their own authors (so did everyone else) and patronized their own painters. Since hard work, perseverance, thrift, and honesty seemed always to be rewarded, they clung to the old virtues. They were materialistic. Gregarious, they gathered at their own lodges and clubs and churches. They enjoyed their politics, their church suppers, their family reunions, their school exercises, their folklore, their recreations—in short, life as they found it. Perhaps their horizon was low. Those young men who went east to college frequently came back to live in Indiana. "Making it" in New York City was no more challenging than making it in Indianapolis. No one was ashamed to be known as a Hoosier; in fact, it was a badge of honor. They knew who they were and what they were, and thus they were stable.

After 1920, influences appeared that tended to mould Hoosiers into the national pattern and chip away their distinctive traits. Mobility, from automobiles and good roads, loosened inhabitants from their isolated localities and encouraged travel to the cities and out of the state. Yet Americans focused on their own problems and pleasures, ignoring the rest of the world. As much as any other factor, increased mobility undermined the country church and church affiliation in general. With movies and radio and amusement parks and auto racing, entertainment became commercial and the same for all, all over the country. The Depression was a common experience, and unions spread out from the Calumet industries. There was a turn to state government, and then to the federal government for relief. It was a blow to self-reliance and to the faith that the economic environment, unlike the weather, was not capricious and not without corrective laws.

The second World War was another sad, anxious, unifying experience. Isolationism was reduced. The united effort to serve and win brought together the people who had been parted by the Depression. Employment was general and rising. Indiana was doing something visible and significant; the old feeling of equality returned. Rising confidence brightened the postwar horizon. College enrollments ballooned here as elsewhere. New industries moved into Indiana, bringing both managers and workers from other states, diluting the native population. The spread of television had everyone watching the same network shows, familiar with the same entertainments, hearing the same songs and jokes. With a stronger economy, optimism reasserted itself.

In the early 1950s, when Senator Joseph McCarthy's witch hunt for Communists was echoed by former Communists beating their breasts over having seen the true light at last, when liberals were mourning the passing of freedom, and British historian Arnold Toynbee was concluding a pessimistic appraisal of the survival of Western civilization, the clear, cool Hoosier voice of Elmer Davis was raised. He was disgusted by all extremists. The country was not doomed this way or that, because the extremists were blind to the vast indistinct area between the clear-cut choices they insisted upon. Davis knew there were numerous people in between who subscribed to neither doctine. They believed simply in trying to find a way, hoping to do their best; not just muddling through, but holding the fabric of society together. But neither Communists nor former Communists have any patience with experimental thinking; they want a final truth and they insist that they possess it.[1] Davis was speaking for the unimpressed: the Hoosiers—and the millions of people like them in other states—who had grown tired of Senator Jenner's support of McCarthy and who knew empty rattling when they heard it. And they did prevail over the doom-sayers.

President James Conant of Harvard once said that the right to think and question and investigate is the basic difference between the free world and the totalitarian world. Hoosiers have always known that, though they forgot it briefly under the spell of the Klan. Most of the time, they think for themselves. Because of surviving differences between north and south, there are always countervailing forces at work. What one area or one type of worker wants, another opposes. Conflicting interests, different aims, variant energies not only provoke discussion, but

1. Elmer Davis, *But We Were Born Free* (Indianapolis: Bobbs-Merrill Co., 1954), chapter 4.

prevent the state from moving firmly or swiftly in a given direction.

All of these external and internal influences have operated to homogenize the inhabitants of Indiana. They are more exposed to common experiences than they used to be. Those who contend that north and south are growing alike mean that southern Hoosiers are becoming more like those in the north. If the differences seem to have diminished, they have by no means disappeared, and a few observers believe that they have actually increased. There is still evidence of more energy and quickness and impersonal detachment in the north. A revival of interest in the history and traditions of southern Indiana has made that area more conscious of its distinctive heritage. The people remain friendly to visitors, but time is required for new residents from "outside" to gain acceptance by the old elite. The growing number of retired people moving into southern Indiana is giving a new cast to the region, not matched by a similar age group entering the north.

The growth of industry has attracted probably as many southern laborers into northern cities as there are northerners; what it has done in southern Indiana is to introduce labor unions that did not exist earlier. Mediators find the new unionists in the south a tumultuous bunch, likely to turn violent, and as unwilling to obey their elected officials as they are to accommodate their employers. Contract negotiations do not proceed with the same civility that they do in the north. So a flat declaration that Hoosiers are growing more alike cannot be made without challenges. Yet, to select a typical Hoosier today, one would look for him in southern Indiana, simply on the ground that there are fewer "outsiders" in that part of the state.

If Hoosiers feel a state loyalty like that of the inhabitants of Maine, Virginia, and Texas, it is because generally they know something of their own history. National patriotism is more critical. It is rooted in a feeling for land, for the expansive nation, for the continental potential, rather than enthusiasm for the federal government. Hoosiers actually don't care much for their

Uncle Sam: Indiana newspapers carp about the extravagance of the government in Washington, its welfare generosity and foreign aid, its foolish programs and bumbling bureaucracy, which intrude on state and private affairs. Indianans complain about contributing a dollar in federal taxes and getting back only seventy-three cents in federal expenditures. Only four other states obtain less, while states in the South and Southwest receive more: Arizona gets back $1.41, and New Mexico $1.93. The notion of being plucked for the benefit of others rankles most Hoosiers, year after year. Yet they also resent offers of federal grants to education and housing, because of strings attached. They observe November 11 as Veterans Day, not the October Monday decreed by Congress. They have opposed the imposition of seasonal daylight-saving time. They prefer to go their own way.

One reason they can afford to pursue their own course is that Indiana has been singularly blessed by the philanthropy of a few local families, as much as any state and more than most. Not that those families were so extraordinarily rich, but they affectionately confined their bounty within the state. Without that private help, Indiana would be straitened, especially in higher education.

Chauncey Rose (1794–1877), who came to Terre Haute in 1818 and made a fortune as a railroad builder, gave money to the local Normal School, to Wabash College, and finally to a local technical school founded in 1874, the first private engineering college west of the Alleghenies. After his death, the school was renamed Rose Polytechnic Institute. His generosity has been matched by gifts from Anton Hulman, Jr., Terre Haute businessman and owner of the Indianapolis Motor Speedway. Today the college is known as the Rose-Hulman Institute.

John Herron's bequest to the Art Association of Indianapolis has been mentioned. The Indianapolis Foundation began quietly in 1916 as a local trust fund to which anyone and everyone might contribute. It received a large increase in 1932 through incorporation of the William E. English Foundation under the same trustees. The English bequest was used to construct a building that houses twenty-seven charitable agencies and pays for depreciation and part of maintenance. As a result, those agencies have only small overhead costs for office space. The Indianapolis Foundation has handed out more than $13 million to local agencies, while it continues to grow from bequests and gifts. Its present assets are $16 million.

The Ball brothers of Muncie established a foundation in 1926 with current assets of $19 million. It concentrates on local giving, with emphasis on Ball State University, hospitals, churches, and civic improvements.

The Irwin-Sweeney-Miller Foundation in Columbus has a capital of $23 million and devotes the interest to programs in racial and social justice, religion, education, and the arts. The Krannert Charitable Trust in Indianapolis is nearly as large and has been especially generous to Purdue University (the Krannert Graduate School of Management), the University of Evansville, Hanover College, the Indianapolis Museum of Art (Krannert Pavilion), the Indiana University Hospital, and the Methodist Hospital of Indianapolis.

Then there is the Lilly Endowment, which made grants amounting to $53 million nationally in 1975. Since its modest establishment in 1937, it has expended $150 million in Indiana alone on the private colleges, the Indiana Historical Society, the Lilly Library, New Harmony restoration, church programs, charities, and recreations. This huge sum is quite apart from the enormous benefactions of members of the Lilly family on local projects, which far exceed that figure.

Taken all together, this munificence has enabled Indiana institutions to achieve stability, to reach more people, to serve more effectively, and to be independent in whole or in part of government grants. Hoosiers prefer to look after themselves. There is a noticeable lack of flashy, personal extravagance among wealthy families. Wealth is often indiscernible, for the richest seldom flaunt it. Such persons invariably consider themselves as middle-class, part of the general effort to be average, rather than exceptional. It is that attitude that causes Hoosiers to resent arrogance and not allow temperament among the most talented.

Although they like gadgets, yet the things that man makes do not seem to take charge of his life. What a person *is* still counts for more than what he has or what he does.

Today some Hoosiers consider themselves liberals—yet, may not be. Others do not hesitate to call themselves conservatives. Both are contemptuous of radicals and reactionaries. Both are vaguely aware that the difference between them is primarily one of degree. Basically, both types prize individualism, even while viewing each other with suspicion. That is, the liberals accuse the conservatives of favoring the strongest individuals at the expense of community interest. The conservatives counterattack by accusing the liberals of sacrificing the good of the community to protect the oddest, most irresponsible members. Actually, both antagonists distrust society, blaming it for corrupting individual members or forcing them toward collectivism for the common good.

If Indiana exhibits a conservative stance in politics, economics, religion, and social concerns (and some astute observers insist that moderates have recently routed the conservatives), she has not come to that position from ignorance or innocence, but from broad experience. This explanation of the present as shaped and sustained by the past is not well understood, even in Indiana. She has witnessed an educative procession of novel, varied, and experimental communities and political parties. She has tolerated illiteracy, bigotry, and political dishonesty longer than she should have before making corrections. She has endured wars, panics, and depressions. Once she spent money wildly. These experiences have been largely forgotten by the current generation, but they all helped to sharpen Hoosier values and choices. Experimentation ultimately lost its appeal and came under suspicion; was it really necessary to try everything anyone suggested? Folk wisdom seemed more reliable: the tried and true was more comfortable. It was not a case of bitter disillusionment and rejection of change, but of deliberate discrimination, a sign of growing sophistication that non-Hoosiers seldom perceive.

Admittedly, it is difficult today to sell a new idea to the general assembly, a chamber of commerce, a newspaper, a church congregation, or a union. Hoosier minds are not closed, but they are wary. Changes are effected only by small steps. Whether this cautious pace may be ascribed to ingrained skepticism or to penetrating intelligence is for someone else to argue. Let me only suggest that it may be owing to a dim recollection of having tried something similar long ago.

That unhurried way of looking at things is significant in the 1970s in the face of the sociological "futurists." They are alarmed at the rate of change in our culture. It is moving too fast, they say; people cannot adjust, there will come a "future shock." The academics are attracted to this cheerless diagnosis. What Alvin Toffler and his sort overlook, however, are people like the Hoosiers. They don't swing with the fads, they don't rush to adopt new concepts or accept new techniques. They don't panic, but serve as national stabilizers and as a powerful brake on change. They can live in juxtaposition to new notions for a long time, until those views that don't founder become as familiar as their own homes. Gradually and belatedly, Hoosiers adjust. Though they disgust impatient reformers, they avoid cultural shocks. They are not passengers in a car careening out of control, but sit in the driver's seat and slowly roll along.

Perhaps they have the vices of their virtues. They may, for instance, be a little too self-satisfied in their conservatism, a little too shallow in their materialism, somewhat undiscriminating in their taste for literature and art, a little too undemanding in their standards of education. But over the long haul, I will bet on them to survive—with grace.

Suggestions for Further Reading

Indiana has been fortunate in the quality and quantity of her historians, beginning with John Scott, who compiled *The Indiana Gazetteer, or Topographical Dictionary* (Centerville, Ind.: John Scott, Printer, 1826). The first orthodox history of the state was the work of Logansport editor John B. Dillon, *The History of Indiana from Its Earliest Exploration by Europeans to . . . 1816 . . .* (Indianapolis: Published by W. Sheets & Co., for J. B. Dillon and S. Lasselle, 1843). Of the several multivolume histories of the state, published between 1903 and 1954, and prepared by William Henry Smith, William M. Cockrum, Jacob P. Dunn, Professor Charles Roll, Professor Logan Esarey, and professors John D. Barnhart and Donald F. Carmony, the best is still being written. It is sponsored jointly by the Indiana Historical Society and the Indiana Historical Bureau, and three of the five volumes have appeared so far: *Indiana to 1816, the Colonial Period*, by John D. Barnhart and Dorothy L. Riker, 1971; *Indiana in the Civil War Era, 1850–1880*, by Emma Lou Thornbrough, 1965; and *Indiana in Transition, the Emergence of an Industrial Commonwealth, 1880–1920*, by Clifton J. Phillips, 1968. Amid this proliferation, nothing has superseded the Writers Program, Work Projects Administration's *Indiana, a Guide to the Hoosier State* (New York: Oxford University Press, 1941); it is a guide with many rare bits of local information. R. L. Baker and Marvin Carmony trace the origins of *Indiana Place Names* (Bloomington: 1975).

R. C. Buley's *The Old Northwest, Pioneer Period, 1815–1840*, (Indianapolis: Indiana Historical Society, 1950), which won the Pulitzer Prize in history in 1951, contains much on early Indiana. Two volumes of travel accounts by visitors to Indiana have appeared: *Indiana as Seen by Early Travelers* (Indianapolis: Indiana Historical Commission, 1916), edited by Harlow Lindley, and *Travel Accounts of Indiana, 1679–1961* (Indianapolis: Indiana Historical Bureau, 1970), edited by Shirley S. McCord.

Particular studies are not wanting, and several are mentioned in the footnotes. Stephen S. Visher has described the *Climate of Indiana* (Bloomington: Indiana University, 1944), and Charles C. Deam has written on the trees, shrubs, and flowers of the state. The earliest inhabitants are the subject of Eli Lilly's *Prehistoric Antiquities of Indiana* (Indianapolis: Indiana Historical Society, 1937) and Glenn A. Black's *Angel Site* (Indianapolis: Indiana Historical Society, 1967). The role of Indiana in the War for Independence is best covered in George M. Waller's *The American Revolution in the West* (Chicago: Nelson-Hall, 1976). Indispensable to any survey of art and architecture are two books by Wilbur D. Peat: *Pioneer Painters of Indiana* (Indianapolis: Art Association of Indianapolis, 1954) and *Indiana Houses of the Nineteenth Century* (Indianapolis: Indiana Historical Society, 1962). The output of Hoosier authors is examined in Meredith Nicholson's *The Hoosiers* (New York: Macmillan, 1900), in Arthur W. Shumaker's *A History of Indiana Literature* (Indianapolis: Indiana Historical Society, 1962), in R. E. Banta's *Indiana Authors and Their Books, 1816–1916* (Crawfordsville: Wabash College, 1949), and in Donald E. Thompson's *Indiana Authors and Their Books, 1916–1966* (Crawfordsville: Wabash College, 1974). Banta has also prepared an anthology of Indiana writings in *Hoosier Caravan* (Bloomington: Indiana University Press, 1975).

Harmony and New Harmony have been treated lightly in *The Ohio,* Rivers of America Series (New York: Holt, Rinehart and Winston, 1949), by R. E. Banta, probingly in *The Wabash* (New York: Farrar & Rinehart, 1940) and *The Angel and the Serpent: The Story of New Harmony* (Bloomington: Indiana University Press, 1964) by William E. Wilson, and philosophically in *Backwoods Utopias* (Philadelphia: University of Pennsylvania Press, 1950) by Arthur E. Bestor. Most of the colleges and universities have had their histories published in book form. As for the early development of primary and secondary schools, Richard G. Boone's *A History of Education in Indiana* (New York: R. Appleton and Co., 1892) is still standard. Similarly, almost every church denomination in Indiana has its chronicler. William C. Latta wrote an *Outline History of Indiana Agriculture* (Lafayette: Purdue University and Indiana County Agricultural Agents Association, 1938), and George W. Starr studied *Industrial Development of Indiana* (Bloom-

ington: School of Business Administration, Indiana University, 1937).
J. A. Batchelor focused on one resource in *An Economic History of the Indiana Oolitic Limestone Industry* (Bloomington: Indiana University School of Business, 1944). World War II experiences are related in *Letters from Fighting Hoosiers* (Bloomington: Indiana War History Commission, 1948), edited by Howard H. Peckham and Shirley Snyder. The best account of state and local government is to be found in the state Chamber of Commerce's booklet, *Here is Your Indiana Government* (Indianapolis: Indiana Chamber of Commerce, 1975). In sports, two books make good reading: Al Bloemker's *500 Miles to Go: The Story of the Indianapolis Speedway* (New York: Coward-McCann, 1961) and Herb Schwomeyer's *Hoosier Hysteria* (Greenfield: n.p., 1975) about high school basketball.

Every county has had its history written, and so has an occasional city. Two fascinating accounts of Indianapolis are Jeannette C. Nolan's *Hoosier City, the Story of Indianapolis* (New York: Julian Messner, 1943) and Charlotte Cathcart's *Indianapolis from Our Old Corner* (Indianapolis: Indiana Historical Society, 1965). Both the Indiana Historical Society and the Indiana Historical Bureau have for decades published reputable and solid studies of various aspects of state history, as well as basic documents. Lists of their titles may be obtained from their offices in the State Library and Historical Building, Indianapolis. And, of course, the *Indiana Magazine of History* at Bloomington has carried articles on state history since 1904.

In the last thirty years, three very good interpretations of the state have been published. John Bartlow Martin provided an excellent postwar picture, based on extensive interviews, in *Indiana, an Interpretation* (New York: A. A. Knopf, 1947). Irving Leibowitz, one-time Indianapolis newspaperman, offered his views of the state in *My Indiana* (Englewood Cliffs, N.J.: Prentice-Hall, 1964). William E. Wilson, Indiana University novelist and professor of English, reviewed his home state in *Indiana, a History* (Bloomington: Indiana University Press, 1966). They are thoughtful and observant authors. An anthology of this nature, in which sixteen writers gave their views on as many aspects of state history, was edited by Donald F. Carmony as *Indiana, a Self-Appraisal* (Bloomington: Indiana University Press, 1966).

Index